CLOSING
THE GAP

*Digital Equity Strategies
for the K–12 Classroom*

SARAH THOMAS, NICOL R. HOWARD, REGINA SCHAFFER

International Society for Technology in Education
PORTLAND, OREGON • ARLINGTON, VIRGINIA

Praise for *Closing the Gap*

"This book is a must-read for all educators implementing digital literacy in schools and classrooms. The authors provide an overarching framework of what's at stake when it comes to digital equity and why we should all care about creating an inclusive digital learning environment."

> — Rusul Alrubail, executive director, Parkdale Centre for Innovation, and an author, speaker, and social justice advocate

"*Closing the Gap* is a timely, methodical, and accessible approach to the current unequally distributed use of edtech in schools. This book addresses the entire spectrum of what leaders need to improve their educational and edtech ecosystems. Based on the ISTE Standards and with real life anecdotes, it's easy to read and powerful to implement the suggestions in *Closing the Gap*."

> — Jon Corippo, CUE chief learning officer and co-author of *The Eduprotocol Field Guide*

"While many of us who work with educational technology would agree on the need for digital equity, there are few comprehensive resources that deal with the practical implications of striving for equitable tech use in K–12 classrooms. As such, this timely and accessible book addresses a key gap in the existing literature."

> — Alec Couros, Ph.D., professor of educational technology and media, University of Regina, Saskatchewan, Canada

"*Closing the Gap* is an enlightening resource for every educational stakeholder in pursuit of equity and access for children. Not only do the authors define digital equity and identify problems of practice, but they offer research, make recommendations for implementation, and address future implications. Teachers, coaches, and school leaders will truly make an impact when equipped with this information. If you're interested in closing opportunity gaps and creating equitable teaching and learning opportunities, including digital equity, *Closing the Gap* is the perfect resource for you."

> — Rosa Isiah, Ed.D., director, elementary education, Norwalk-La Mirada Unified School District

"This book should be essential reading for all educators. It identifies a largely unrecognized issue in modern education and thoughtfully lays out clear and actionable steps to address it. Authors Thomas, Howard, and Schaffer make clear that issues of equity impact all of our students and we're all responsible for closing the gap."

— Jennie Magiera, chief program officer, EdTechTeam, and author of *Courageous Edventures: Navigating Obstacles to Discover Classroom Innovation*

"*Closing the Gap* shines a spotlight on one of today's largest educational issues—digital equity. Authors Thomas, Howard, and Schaffer will guide you in identifying, analyzing, and problem-solving these disparities, while bringing to light that these solutions are not simply things we can do—but things *we must do*. Providing equity in access and equity in opportunity is a moral imperative for today's educators, and this book provides the needed tools, resources, stories from the field, and practical suggestions to make it happen!"

— Thomas C. Murray, director of innovation, Future Ready Schools, and author of *Learning Transformed: 8 Keys to Designing Tomorrow's Schools, Today*

"Technology in the hands of teachers who deeply care about their students' learning is powerful. This book provides solutions and real-life examples for these teachers who desperately want to help their students who are most in need of access."

— Shelly Sanchez Terrell, digital innovator, author, and teacher

"*Closing the Gap* should be on every desk of every school leader who needs a valuable resource for not just bridging the digital and achievement gaps in their district/school board, but closing those gaps. There are real tangible examples with a framework for a sustainable plan. The examples are also from actual practitioners and not from people who haven't done, or are not actively doing, the work."

— Ken Shelton, global keynote specialist and educational technology strategist for EdTechTeam

"Kudos for a guide that addresses the preparation, actions, and support necessary for digital equity. Based on research and day-to-day classroom experiences, *Closing the Gap* is a practical guide with clear explanations, examples, and recommendations. The result in an excellent resource for any educator—classroom teacher, coach, or administrator."

— Adina Sullivan-Marlow, K–12 educational technology coordinator and founder of EquityEDU

Closing the Gap
Digital Equity Strategies for the K–12 Classroom
Sarah Thomas, Nicol R. Howard, Regina Schaffer

Acquisitions Editor: *Valerie Witte*
Developmental and Copy Editor: *Linda Laflamme*
Proofreader: *Steffi Drewes*
Indexer: *Wendy Allex*
Book Design and Production: *Kim McGovern*
Cover Design: *Edwin Ouellette*

Library of Congress Cataloging-in-Publication Data available

First Edition
ISBN: 9781564847171

Ebook version available

Printed in the United States of America

ISTE® is a registered trademark of the International Society for
Technology in Education.

About ISTE

The International Society for Technology in Education (ISTE) is a nonprofit organization that works with the global education community to accelerate the use of technology to solve tough problems and inspire innovation. Our worldwide network believes in the potential technology holds to transform teaching and learning.

ISTE sets a bold vision for education transformation through the ISTE Standards, a framework for students, educators, administrators, coaches and computer science educators to rethink education and create innovative learning environments. ISTE hosts the annual ISTE Conference & Expo, one of the world's most influential edtech events. The organization's professional learning offerings include online courses, professional networks, year-round academies, peer-reviewed journals and other publications. ISTE is also the leading publisher of books focused on technology in education. For more information or to become an ISTE member, visit iste.org. Subscribe to ISTE's YouTube channel and connect with ISTE on Twitter, Facebook and LinkedIn.

Related ISTE Titles

Closing the Gap: Digital Equity Strategies for Teacher Prep Programs

Nicol R. Howard, Sarah Thomas, Regina Schaffer

To see all books available from ISTE, please visit iste.org/resources.

About the Authors

Sarah Thomas, PhD, is a Regional Technology Coordinator in Prince George's County Public Schools. She is also a Google Certified Innovator, Google Education Trainer, and the founder of the EduMatch movement, a project that empowers educators to make global connections across common areas of interest. She has presented internationally, has participated in the Technical Working Group to refresh the 2017 ISTE Standards for Educators, and is a recipient of the 2017 ISTE Making IT Happen award. Dr. Thomas is also a national advisor for the Future Ready Instructional Coaches Strand and an Affiliate Professor at Loyola University in Maryland.

Nicol R. Howard, PhD, is an Assistant Professor in the School of Education at the University of Redlands. She has served as co-chair for ISTE's Digital Equity Network; chair of the American Educational Research Association's Technology, Instruction, Cognition, and Learning SIG; and co-chair for the California Council on Teacher Education (CCTE) Technology SIG. Her research foci are teacher education, STEM, and computer science opportunities for students of color, as well as the equitable uses of technology in K–16 classrooms. Her writing has appeared in the *Urban Education Journal; International Journal of Educational Technology; Technology, Knowledge and Learning;* the Corwin Connected Educators Series; EDUCAUSE; Edutopia; and eCampus News. She is also the co-founder and co-editor of the *Journal of Computer Science Integration.*

Dr. Howard holds a Bachelor's Degree in Sociology from the University of California at Los Angeles (UCLA), an MA in Educational Technology from Azusa Pacific University, and a PhD in Cultural and Curricular Studies from Chapman University. She is also a Google Education Trainer, a Microsoft Innovative Educator Trainer, and Raspberry Pi Certified.

 **Regina Schaffer** is a Technology Specialist for the Middletown Township School District. She has served as co-chair for ISTE's Digital Equity Network. Her passion for integrating technology in learning for students has been an integral part of her evolution as a modern educator. She is an advocate for using technology to bridge the gaps that exist for many of our nation's students. As a teacher, Regina used technology to support high standards in a learner-centered classroom. Through the use of Problem-Based Inquiry and Experiential models, Regina designed and facilitated technology-infused learning experiences that provided students with real-world context, while promoting the academic independence that nurtures them as lifelong learners. She is part of a district-level connected educator team that helps facilitate the district's vision as they continue to evolve as a community of educators committed to preparing students for their future. Regina was recently selected as a National School Boards Association's "20 to Watch," as well as a 2016 PBS LearningMedia Digital Innovator. She is a Future Ready National Thought Leader, Google Certified Innovator, Common Sense Media Certified Teacher, Discovery Education DEN Star, Remind Connected Educator, BrainPOP Connected Educator, Raspberry Pi Certified Educator, and PBL Learning Media Digital Innovator. Connect with Regina at @reginaschaffer.

Acknowledgments

We are three authors who connected through our work with ISTE, from across the country, all with a desire to encourage more meaningful efforts at narrowing the digital equity gap. We are thankful for the opportunity to author this second book in our series, and we are grateful for Valerie Witte's guidance throughout this journey as well as the support of ISTE's Digital Equity Leadership Team from 2016 to present.

Special thanks to our contributors: Chris Aviles, George Barcenas, Nichole Carter, Candy Coffey, Cicely Day, Dr. Josue Falaise, Abbey Futrell, Doug Havard, Matthew Hiefield, Carla Jefferson, Valerie Lewis, Kim Roberson, and Dr. Lisa Spencer.

Dedication

Thank you to my family. You are my everything. "Yay, yay, they are great." Much love always.

 —Sarah

To my husband Keith and my children Micaela and Kamau for their love and inspiration. To my bonus son Dwan, daughter-in-love Domunique, and grandson Nahz for encouragement. To my parents DeEtta, Beverly, Joseph, and James, thank you for planting the seeds.

 —Nicol

Special thank you to the late Georgina Lomax, my aunt, whose dedication to education has been and continues to be my inspiration as an educator.

 —Regina

Contents

INTRODUCTION

What comes to mind when you hear the term *digital equity*? Perhaps you're thinking of access to devices, high-speed internet, or high-profile issues like the homework gap and participation gap. If so, you are correct; however, there are nuances to this term and the ways in which different stakeholders have addressed digital equity issues. *Closing the Gap: Digital Equity Strategies for the K–12 Classroom* is one resource that will help guide your efforts in pursuit of digital equity on your campus.

What's in This Book

In Chapter 1, we begin by laying the groundwork to discuss *digital equity*, establishing a common definition and a direction for the book. We then focus on how to resolve *problems of practice*, including assembling a team, identifying and analyzing the problem, and implementing a plan to attack challenges to digital equity. Finally, we set the tone for what will appear in future chapters.

Chapter 2 is all about how teachers can help promote digital equity. Here, we examine the interplay between the International Society for Technology in Education Standards for Educators and those for Students, looking closely at three common themes: lifelong learning, communication, and transforming learning.

Chapter 3 focuses on professional learning. Here, we invite you to circle back to the problem of practice discussed in Chapter 1, and we offer questions for self-evaluation when determining options for professional learning. We also discuss options for self-directed professional learning.

Finally, in Chapter 4, we discuss next steps in the field, specifically addressing school and district leaders. We review suggestions from the Consortium for School Networking (CoSN) and the National Education Technology Plan (NETP), including hotspots, low-cost broadband, and building private networks.

Throughout the book, you will see evidence-based solutions from such organizations as ISTE, Future Ready, and CoSN. You will also find vignettes and DE wisdom from educators in the field. Our hope is that, through a balance of theory and practical examples, you all will be inspired to take action to promote digital equity in your spheres of influence.

Who This Book Is For

Although the target audience of our first book was primarily teacher educators and providers of professional learning opportunities, this book is specifically for teachers (Chapter 2) and coaches (Chapter 3). Additionally, Chapter 4 is geared toward school leaders. One theme that will recur throughout the book is that there is no clear line between these roles. For example, a classroom teacher may serve on the school's technology leadership team and provide after-school workshops for colleagues. We encourage all educational stakeholders to read, participate, and learn with us, as we collectively continue our work to solve digital inequities in education.

Don't forget to show your work using the hashtag #DigEquityBook. Feel free to reach out to us to share your thoughts.

Best,

Sarah (@Sarahdateechur), Nicol (@NicolRHoward), and Regina (@ReginaSchaffer)

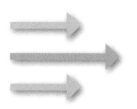

Chapter 1

WHAT WE KNOW ABOUT DIGITAL EQUITY

*As devices and increased bandwidth have improved, we are now
seeing the next great equity challenge: the way educators use
technology with their students. An emerging definition of digital
equity now involves access to devices, access to broadband,
and access to teachers qualified to offer technology-powered
opportunities to drive learning in the classroom.*

—Hiefield & Carter, 2018

Do you remember the first time you ever used a computer
for learning new content? Did you have your own device,
or did you go to the local library? What about your Wi-Fi
connectivity? More than likely, the answers to these
questions vary from reader to reader just as they differ
amongst K–12 students today. Challenges related to
device access, bandwidth, and Wi-Fi connectivity persist,
yet these are not the only concerns related to digital
equity in K–12 classrooms. Digital equity is also inclusive of the selection and application of digital tools in
teaching and learning. To that end, we are long overdue

for change beyond simply the distribution of more devices (Howard, Thomas, & Schaffer, 2018).

Digital equity is not a new term, yet differing beliefs and practices continue to emerge related to this topic. In the first book of this series, *Closing the Gap: Digital Equity Strategies for Teacher Prep Programs*, the authors addressed how researchers have defined digital equity as "equal access and opportunity to digital tools, resources, and services to increase digital knowledge, awareness, and skills" (Davis, Fuller, Jackson, Pittman, & Sweet, 2007, p.1). Digital equity is most visible when everyone, including teachers, coaches, and K–12 students, have adequate access to technologies for teaching and learning *and* when those digital teaching and learning experiences are well-designed and delivered. The mere replication of paper-based lessons via easily accessible digital tools is not enough, however; we must strive for better and richer experiences by supporting those who provide them to students.

When digital technologies are used in instruction, teaching and learning experiences still differ between classrooms based upon numerous factors including, but not limited to, teacher beliefs and their prior experiences with learning and using new technologies. When teachers have had positive and interactive experiences learning a new tool, their educational application of that tool will produce far more positive experiences for their students as well. Teachers who begrudgingly adopt a new digital tool are less likely to feel comfortable using it with their students. A teacher's comfort level with using new technologies can ultimately be traced back to their own learning experiences. We'll discuss this in more depth in Chapter 3, but we raise the issue now to highlight how gaps in teachers' tech knowledge are also a variable to consider when addressing digital inequities.

We can aim to ensure K–12 students have access to devices, Wi-Fi, and digital tools; however, if students do not have a teacher qualified to use technologies equitably, then closing the digital equity gap is less likely to occur. Coach and teacher preparedness for dealing with digital inequities on K–12 campuses is essential for the future success of K–12 students. To address the ongoing issues associated with digital equity, it is important to carefully consider the complexity of the issues and whether they need urgent attention or long-term strategic planning efforts. Whether or not it is determined that any given digital inequity requires immediate resolution, a process for determining the plan for solving the problem is essential.

Problem of Practice

Similar to other areas a school or school district may identify as a core focus, issues related to digital equity can be considered a *problem of practice*. Digital inequities are a problem of practice because of their instructional impacts, directly observable issues (e.g., poor Wi-Fi connectivity), potential for improvement, and connections to a larger strategic plan. There are a few essential steps to closing the digital equity gap that are vital as you address your problem of practice. The goal for this chapter is to support you with navigating this process of *identifying, analyzing*, and *planning for teaching and learning around* your own or your district's problem of practice related to digital equity. We will break down each phase of the process in an effort to help you facilitate this same process related to identifying and addressing digital inequities on your own campus. Why is it important to identify and address problems of practice? Focusing on solving a clear problem of practice can lead to cultural changes and student success. Let's walk through the process using some examples of complex and urgent digital equity concerns that require teachers and coaches to consider how they will ensure equity for all.

Who Is on Your Team?

Before identifying the problem of practice, you should highly consider approaching the challenges with a team or determine a group of colleagues to at least bounce around a few solution-based ideas. For example, if you are a teacher, you could seek out your technology coach, a teacher on special assignment (TOSA), a peer educator, and even students on your campus. Bouncing around ideas may be as simple as a holding a face-to-face meeting in which your team comes together one time to brainstorm the issues and possible solutions. You could even follow-up with a shared space for collecting additional afterthoughts using a digital platform (e.g., Padlet, Google Docs). Whether you meet face-to-face or online, part of your team's work will involve unpacking the challenges to better understand:

- The root cause of any given issue
- What can be solved through a shift in digital equity strategies (e.g., full 1:1 access)
- What steps your team can take toward supporting K–12 students as well as each other

A team approach, whenever possible, may potentially lead to schoolwide improvements and the identification of issues that broadly impact a campus—even when the initial general assumption was that only one classroom was impacted by digital inequities. If you are addressing a problem of practice alone, you may find support by leaning on your larger community of practice, also known as your professional learning network (PLN), which we discuss further in Chapter 3.

Identifying the Specific Problem

When identifying the specific problem of practice, your team could take the brainstorm approach and lay out every digital equity challenge on the campus. Alternatively, one person could bring a key concern to the group. Although you may have picked up this book with one key concern on your mind, take a moment to think again about your role in education and your own personal digital equity challenges. Whether you are a K–12 teacher or a coach, you are likely facing a digital inequity on your campus at varying degrees. Perhaps it is an inequity related to poor Wi-Fi connectivity or outdated operating systems. Maybe you lack enough devices to work efficiently with students or colleagues on a project. Obvious gaps may even exist in the digital knowledge between teachers and students, coaches and teachers, or peer teachers and students. There could be inequities evident between classrooms due to the varying uses of digital tools for teaching and learning, such as one teacher using technology for drill-and-kill practice exercises and another using digital tools for collaboration and deeper learning.

Allow the results of this fresh brainstorming to help inform your process for identifying the most pressing digital inequity in your classroom or on your campus. Remember that this stage of the process may begin with your own thoughts, yet it is important to solicit the perspective of other key stakeholders (e.g., colleagues, students) to prioritize the challenges that require immediate attention. Your team may decide to take a divide-and-conquer approach by having every member identify one challenge to address, or you may decide to tackle them as a group, one challenge at a time. Whichever approach the team takes, you must analyze the problem of practice in order to appropriately plan for teaching and learning.

Analyzing the Problem

After your team identifies a problem of practice as the one challenge you will tackle, it is time to carefully analyze that problem. For example, if your team determines that the most pressing challenge is the disparity between how digital tools are used between classrooms for teaching and learning, begin to unpack the issue as a team and discuss the root causes. Key data points should be utilized to make this determination, such as student surveys and parent feedback, or observable differences in teaching with technology and the acquisition of new knowledge when using technology for teaching and learning.

The goal in this process is to determine *which* problems can be solved through a shift in digital equity strategies; the *how* occurs during the next phase. While analyzing the problem of practice, your team should continue to consider all of the key stakeholders (e.g., students, parents, colleagues) in order to prepare to develop a clear plan for teaching and learning. Analyze the problem from the perspective of each stakeholder to best understand the root causes of the issue. In the example above about the disparities between how digital tools may be used between classrooms, your team might examine the impact on both student learning and teacher autonomy. Or one of your team members, likely the coach, might be called upon to observe frequency and types of technology use in different classrooms for the team to compare and further analyze together. The team may discover that although the problem was labeled as a disparity in use, a closer look reveals that there is not actually a difference in how the tool is used, rather a difference in *how often* the tool is used and the root cause is the teacher's discomfort managing the classroom when technology use is a variable. Once the problem has been analyzed and the root cause determined, your team is ready to plan for teaching and learning.

An Organizational Tool for Brainstorming and Analyzing

The International Technology and Engineering Educators Association (ITEEA) defines the design process as, "a systematic problem-solving strategy, with criteria and constraints, used to develop many possible solutions to a problem or to satisfy human needs and wants and winnow (narrow) down the possible solutions to one final choice" (n.d.). The organization has developed a twelve-step Engineering Design Process (EDP) for use in Grades 9–12, which Thomas (n.d.) repurposed as "Designing with Passion," an activity for educators to develop a plan to attack their own problems of practice.

The activity uses Google Forms (bit.ly/DesignWithPassion) to guide you through the first six steps of the EDP: Define the problem, brainstorm possible solutions, research ideas/explore possibilities, specify constraints, consider alternatives, and select an approach. Once the form is completed, you will receive an email containing a Google Docs document with the information that was initially supplied, plus a section to address the final six steps of the process. This latter section includes places to add due dates and resources to guide you along the way. The Google Docs document is also added to a community database (databases.edumatch.org/designingwithpassion) where educators can go to search for similar plans to gain ideas on what to do or to find potential collaborators. A template of the document for private use is available at getconnected.edumatch.org/dwptemplate.

▲ ▲ ▲

Planning for Teaching and Learning

Perhaps the assumption may be that this stage of the process is the fastest to maneuver, when in actuality now is when new questions and digital inequities emerge that you will explore and address. The beauty of this process is that we, all educators, already know careful *planning* for teaching and learning benefits students tremendously. We embrace the process. Acknowledging new inequities and seeking to answer emerging questions better prepares educators to meet the needs of all students. Working alongside a colleague, or with a team, will help, but this work can be done alone. For now, we will offer an example using a team approach. Continuing with the example scenario, your team might plan to connect coaches with teachers to support them with managing their classrooms during lessons that require 1:1 device distribution and the use of new digital tools. Or, your team might decide to offer teachers some professional learning that goes over new ways to manage tech-centered classrooms. Although it may feel like a long way to get to this final step, here is where your team potentially transforms education and empowers both students and teachers (Figure 1.1).

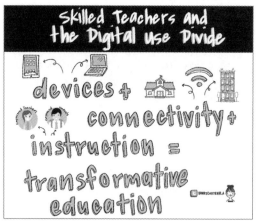

Figure 1.1 Instruction is an essential part of the equation to achieving digital equity. *(Sketchnote by Nichole Carter.)*

Proper planning for teaching and learning, after identifying and analyzing the problem of practice, cannot occur in isolation. In other words, this is an iterative process. Once the *planning for teaching and learning* stage of the cycle is complete, remember to continue collecting data, such as student and teacher reactions to the implementation of plan, to determine whether it may be necessary to revisit one of the stages in the process. Most importantly, remember to embrace the teamwork approach, acknowledging the importance of each group member: teachers, coaches, and campus leaders.

 Educator Voices

What Can Happen When You Address the Problem of Practice

By Candy Coffey, Instructional Technology Coach

The present-day expectation of technology integration is to supplement, enrich, and facilitate 21st-century learning. In accordance with this is the need and desire of our students to have educational experiences with new technologies to prepare them for the future. My school embraced this ideology: At Palm Avenue Elementary School, which is located in the north end of San Bernardino, California, we developed a comprehensive action plan directly aligned to our school's needs. Our plan not only budgeted school funds for a variety of devices, but also employed an expert leader to serve as an instructional technology coach and resource to students, teachers, staff, and the community.

The instructional technology coach's responsibilities include offering consistent availability, mentoring teachers to provide support with instructional needs, sharing ideas, and demonstrating programs aligned with student achievement. These responsibilities are performed through weekly lessons in kindergarten through sixth-grade classrooms for fifty-minute sessions. In addition, monthly meetings are held to collaborate with lower-grade (kindergarten through third) and upper-grade (fourth through sixth) teachers separately with the intent to target their specific needs. Technology uses in classrooms across campus are shared via professional development meetings and highlighted in our weekly news broadcast. This sharing of ideas has served as a reminder of the useful application of technology and has resulted in generating heightened interest and use.

Initially, our expectation of the implementation process was not to have an overnight success; we knew results would take time and tremendous effort. Gradually, background knowledge was carefully constructed and consistent monitoring and scaffolding was set in place, leading to what we, as a staff, deem success in relation to our action plan. The first year was focused on learning how to navigate different devices such as iPads, Dell laptops, Mac laptops, and Chromebooks. At this time, we formed a student technology club to educate students about the manipulation and purpose of devices. The members' most important role was to assist teachers and other students in troubleshooting within the classroom. The second year concentrated on teaching applications and programs that increased student achievement, facilitated learning, and improved student engagement. We extended our focus to include the community in a discussion on how technology can be used to enhance learning. Families were encouraged to check out computers through our school district's digital equity initiative. The third year targeted knowledge enhancement, the development of higher order thinking skills, and the establishment of digital citizenship. We feel that involving and supporting all stakeholders in this transition has proven to be an effective strategy and has collectively helped to maximize technological implementation at our school.

Growing Concerns

Digital equity itself is, of course, a continued concern in K–12 education. Although many districts have implemented plans to ensure that adequate infrastructures and access to devices are in place, it has become clearer that the approach to teaching and learning with digital tools can still vary greatly. Digital citizenship and digital equity are closely linked, and we are now noticing an emerging issue: the *participation gap*. Research on the digital participation divide has centered on access related to the time spent utilizing devices, especially at home. "More specifically, the participation divide refers to the fact that some students are more plugged into an internet culture around creating, connecting with others and giving and receiving feedback around their work" (Hiefield & Monterosa, 2018). Historically reports have indicated that students from high socioeconomic backgrounds have more access at home than students from less advantaged home situations; however, with an increase in the use of smartphones, new reports reveal that students from low socioeconomic backgrounds are in fact experiencing greater access to technology today (U.S. Department of Education, 2009; 2016).

The digital participation gap is a growing concern, because there is still a need to support students with their digital citizenship knowledge and comfort level when immersed in the internet culture while accessing technology at home. Addressing the participation gap can begin in schools by supporting students through the process of learning and creating with technology. Teachers and coaches are on the frontlines when it comes to narrowing the participation gap, but administrators are also key as they provide the necessary support with eliminating certain barriers (e.g., funding for resources, access to new tools, funding for professional learning). That said, we believe in a collaborative approach to addressing digital inequities and we understand the importance of each stakeholder's role in this partnership.

Teachers and coaches can support efforts to narrow the participation gap through their collaborative efforts in developing and offering tech-rich learning experiences on their campuses. Teachers do not need to teach in the same way for students to learn; however, technology should be utilized in transformative ways (Figure 1.2). In fact, a variance in instructional practices across one campus may better prepare K–12 students for their future college experiences. While teachers are in the process of figuring out transformative ways to use various digital tools with their students effectively, coaches can provide encouragement and support. In addition, because coaches may also experience having their own digital equity concerns overlooked when identifying the problem of practice, it is truly a good idea to consider a team approach to solving the digital challenges on K–12 campuses.

Figure 1.2 Emerging technologies and strong Wi-Fi call for transformative practices to narrow the participation gap. *(Sketchnote by Nichole Carter.)*

As new technologies emerge, there is a greater need for both teacher and coach support to ensure equity in the educational application of technologies in K–12 classrooms. It is also important to remember that there are multiple ways to effectively respond to digital equity challenges, which we will address further in the next chapter.

 Educator Voices

Drill and Practice versus Meaningful Learning

by Matthew Hiefield, Digital Curriculum Specialist
Nichole Carter, Innovation Strategist

In the late 1990s and again in 2010, studies showed that "low-income, nonwhite children more often used technology in math class for drill and practice, while affluent white children were more likely to use technology for graphing, problem-solving and other higher-order exercises" (Boser, 2013).

Sociologist Paul Atwell observed in the Connected Learning Alliance Report that even as technology gaps close, a digital-use divide becomes increasingly apparent. Affluent students use the same technologies to support richer forms of learning with greater adult mentorship. The report offers evidence of how inequity persists despite removing technical and economic barriers and despite what we know about the social and cultural forces that determine these inequitable outcomes (Reich & Ito, 2017).

The teaching and use of technology becomes a matter of equity and educational opportunity because using technology to "drill and kill" students for test prep saps the creativity and curiosity out of the classroom environment.

These types of activities contain little or no collaboration and don't allow for research and deeper inquiry skills.

Using technology in this way might appear to help educators manage classroom expectations (e.g. "finish this practice test in the next 40 minutes"), but these types of lessons encourage boredom, dread, and misbehavior and don't support critical thinking.

DE Wisdom

Identifying and analyzing a problem of practice, as well as developing a plan for teaching and learning effectively, should not eliminate the opportunity for teachers and students to have the flexibility to select the apps they believe achieve curricular and/ or learning goals (Howard & Howard, 2017). This process should support making the necessary shifts in educational settings that allow for increased opportunities for teachers and students to voice preferences and to choose the digital tools they learn with best.

Join the conversation on Twitter using #DigEquityBook, and share your solution-based ideas with us.

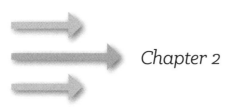

Chapter 2

HOW MIGHT TEACHERS RESPOND TO THE CHALLENGES?

I'm not excited about a world where students just use technology to click through materials on a screen. But I'm very excited about a world where learners use technology to design, create, explore and engage with their peers around the world. This use of technology is incredibly powerful, and it's an opportunity that should be available to everyone.

—Culatta, as quoted in Cortez, 2017

Although a large part of digital equity is access to devices and adequate bandwidth, as we saw in the previous chapter, it is not enough to simply buy devices and pre-packaged programs (such as the "drill-and-kill"). Forcing shiny new technology tools into adoption while the learning and purpose for the integration of the new tool lags behind is no longer an acceptable practice.

Many of us have heard these edtech urban legends, where schools invest tens of thousands of dollars in new devices and programs while leaving the most important part of the equation unsolved: the human factor.

Before rolling out new technology on a large scale, educators must know what to do with it and why the tool was adopted for use. As we mentioned in Chapter 1, the last phase of addressing your digital equity problem of practice is planning for teaching and learning. Proper planning includes professional learning on such topics as tool selection, digital citizenship, student-centered design, facilitation, and more; all of which are all supported by the ISTE Standards for Educators (International Society for Technology in Education [ISTE], 2017).

The ISTE Standards for Students (International Society for Technology in Education [ISTE], 2016) help prepare students for an unknown future, by addressing skills that are gaining importance over time. Shortly, we will discuss this more, but first we'd like to draw attention to the skills we are preparing students to acquire for the future. A good illustration of these, and how they've changed over the decades, can be see in Figure 2.1, which was shared by California educators Adam Juarez and Katherine Goyette in a 2018 presentation at CUE Nevada. As the baby boomers were entering the workforce in 1970, more academic subject-heavy topics were at the top of the list, such as reading, writing, and arithmetic. Nearly fifty years later, however, we see that soft skills have risen as millennials are coming of age. Soft skills will likely continue to play a role in the future workforce, although they often play second fiddle to the core content.

The key approach is to integrate these soft skills seamlessly within the content, as supported by the Standards for Students (ISTE, 2016). Doing so supports learning for all students regardless of learning styles and/or abilities. We are reminded of the work of an ISTE Digital Equity Network Leader, Valerie Lewis, who is currently an assistant principal in Georgia. She recently shared her story with us about the integration of technology in special education (see the sidebar, "Technology in the High School Special Education Setting"). Valerie recognizes that students in special education classrooms are often overlooked, so her refreshing perspective is one we hope you will benefit from hearing.

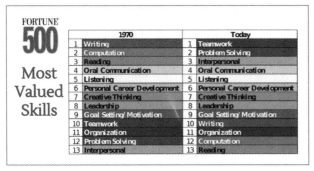

FORTUNE 500 Most Valued Skills	1970	Today
	1 Writing	1 Teamwork
	2 Computation	2 Problem Solving
	3 Reading	3 Interpersonal
	4 Oral Communication	4 Oral Communication
	5 Listening	5 Listening
	6 Personal Career Development	6 Personal Career Development
	7 Creative Thinking	7 Creative Thinking
	8 Leadership	8 Leadership
	9 Goal Setting/Motivation	9 Goal Setting/Motivation
	10 Teamwork	10 Writing
	11 Organization	11 Organization
	12 Problem Solving	12 Computation
	13 Interpersonal	13 Reading

Figure 2.1 Compare the *Fortune 500* list of Most Valued Skills in 1970 and today. *(Image credit: Juarez & Goyette, 2018.)*

 Educator Voices

Technology in the High School Special Education Setting

by Valerie Lewis, Assistant Principal

Learning in and of itself is difficult—not to mention when you are a student diagnosed with learning deficits or more simply, in need of some supports and accommodations.

According to the National Assessment of Educational Progress 12th grade report, 5% of students with disabilities scored at Proficient or beyond in 2011 (Figure 2.2). This certainly does not help our case when pacing guides already send teachers into overdrive. So how does a teacher work around time constraints? What does effective instruction, assessment, and timely feedback look like for students with learning disabilities? After many years in a resource setting, I knew that I had to leverage technology in my classroom, specifically through the effective use of free applications that would complement my classroom instruction.

After you establish your goal, consider how to find the tools that will help you achieve it. Too often people decide that tech is good enough to use without a clear plan. It must serve a purpose. You want to get meaningful work done and not just busy work complete. Every assessment shouldn't just be on paper and pencil—or on a computer. Tech allows students to show what they know in a variety of ways, but more so—it allows access to things and places that may otherwise be considered a stretch. Isn't that what teaching and learning is all about?

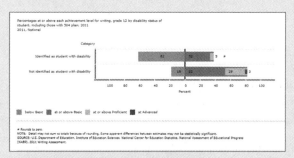

Figure 2.2 Fewer students with disabilities scored at Proficient or beyond *(Image credit: U.S. Dept. of Education, 2011.)*

Writing

For example, writing can be frustrating for students with disabilities because of motor dexterity challenges or because articulating their thoughts through written communication is more difficult. Unfortunately, the curriculum and pacing guides do not often build in the time needed for teachers to model or practice writing. It is still very important for students to write and to recognize writing as not only a form of communication, but also as an important building block to help them develop the necessary skills (e.g., soft skills, motor skills) that will be beneficial beyond writing.

To help students, I integrated Google G Suite (especially Google Docs) into lessons. This tool allowed my students to pull up information and share documents that I could view and edit it in real-time. Chunking students' work or putting it into manageable parts is helpful and perhaps part of the supports or accommodations written in their Individualized Education Plan (IEP). By using Google Docs, my students and I and could easily work on a long essay in chunks, editing them as they were written. This approach not only eliminates the long wait for feedback, but also avoids student frustration and the letdown of having to redo everything after writing a long essay. Both my students and I could gain insight on what they are doing well and what changes would improve their work, as they went along. In the comments section, I could quickly give feedback on capitalization, grammar, sentence structure, word choice or even citing supporting evidence in a research paper. Students would become less anxious when they felt like they were getting individual support along the way and arriving at the end was a whole lot less daunting.

Teaching grammar in isolation is almost a thing of the past. Some teachers find ways to carve out time at the start of class (bell ringer) to complete Daily Grammar Practice (DGP) exercises. Although that approach helps to set a foundation of understanding, some find a less intimidating way to teach this skill through the Grammarly browser extension (grammarly.com). Available for the Chrome, Edge, Firefox, and Safari browsers, this free tool is essentially a writing assistant that helps to spell check, define words, find synonyms, and make timely suggestions while you write. When students are writing, suggestions become visible and they can easily self-correct and then begin to recognize mistakes they often make. You can also have follow-up in conversations with them about their writing ethic and encourage them to goal set and build.

Speaking and Listening

Very rarely do you come across a teen that doesn't have an opinion of his or her own. Under the right context, you just may have a hard time getting them to sit still and quiet. This is where student choice comes in: Topics for discussion (school appropriate, of course) should sometimes come from the students. If they are interested in it, then chances are they are willing to engage and participate. This is half the battle. Too many times, we are dead set on checking off a list of our "must-dos" that we fail to meet the needs of our most important treasure—the students. Find ways in which to connect the units of study, themes, or topics to things that kids like. They may actually retain the understanding much better. Get creative on how you connect standards and skills.

In this age of tech, I don't spend time collecting phones and holding them hostage at the board or behind the door. Instead, I find ways to engage kids with the tech glued to the palm of their hands or other devices they brought to school with them. Through Snapchat, we build Snap Stories, which were reflective of their learning, as well as build #BookSnaps (tarammartin.com/booksnaps-snapping-for-learning).

To tie in the writing component, I also give students the opportunity to pick an area of interest to blog about through

Blogger; being a G Suite for Education school makes this easy. I found my students became most excited when they could get feedback from their peers within the class and those across district, state, and country lines—or out of the country. To push a step further, students also have had the experience of creating their own podcast show using Audacity (sourceforge.net/projects/audacity). Creating intro music, show notes, and a storyboard, as well as researching for evidence that supports their commentary, allows students to use multiple skills across platforms in an authentic way. Just wait until you see what content they can produce! Of course, these are additional ways to assess learning, understanding, or applying the skills you want to see in context.

Reading

Everything circles back to literacy, which is true across all subject areas. Students' Lexile levels are informative on how they can access and understand text. Websites like lexile.com will allow struggling readers more accessibility to information. Do not take for granted the idea that student choice in reading is key. If a student wants to pick up a book and develops a love in that manner, we should celebrate that daily. CommonLit (commonlit.org), Newsela (newsela.com), ReadTheory (readtheory.org), and other online content platforms can assist you in pairing nonfiction, poetry, and current events texts with instruction and standards. I most appreciate that these sites have assessment tools that show student progress in an easy-to-understand manner. This data is shareable with parents and makes having conversations during parent-teacher conferences easier. Working with your media specialists and having them label books, or sections of the library, by Lexile levels is helpful, as well. All of this will help you move the needle towards higher student achievement, while also enabling you to embed such strategies as SOAPStone (speaker, occasion, audience, purpose, subject, tone), RACE (restate the question, answer the question, cite the source, and explain), OPTIC (overview, parts, title, interrelationships, conclusion), and annotating to help students increase meaning and understanding when interacting with text.

Give It a Try
Although this may seem like a lot of suggestions, remember that the new ideas you try will be seamless with practice and time. Find one or two tools to focus on and add to your practice; see how they help inform your understanding of your students' learning and mastery of skills. It is important to continue to grow as an educator and improve your effectiveness through professional knowledge, instruction, communication, assessment uses, and academic rigor. Use tech to leverage what you are doing, but always be clear it will not solve the education gap exclusively.

ISTE Standards

While leveraging technology for learning, be mindful of the role the ISTE Standards can play. They are aspirational, meaning that they are where we would like every student, educator, coach, and administrator to aim as goals on their learning journeys. As for other standards, and even models of technology integration such as SAMR (substitution, augmentation, modification, redefinition) and TPACK (technological pedagogical content knowledge), the point is that our learners should have the capacity to reach these benchmarks, even if they are not evident in every single lesson. Our end goal is certainly an application and a mastery of the ISTE Standards for Students, which can be facilitated by a mastery of the Standards for Educators and Standards for Coaches (ISTE, 2011).

ISTE Standards for Students

The ISTE Standards for Students were first established in 1998, with a focus on learning to use technology. The second iteration in 2007 shifted the lens to using technology for learning. Although not explicitly stated, the ISTE Standards address the digital equity challenges students face today especially through the current version of the Standards, which are centered on transformative learning with technology. The seven standards, shown in Figure 2.3, support the philosophy that

> Today's students must be prepared to thrive in a constantly evolving technological landscape. The ISTE Standards for Students are designed to empower student voice and ensure that learning is a student-driven process. (ISTE, 2016)

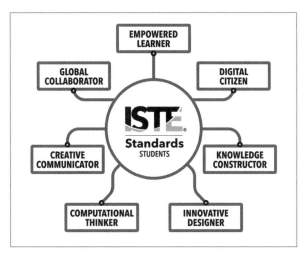

Figure 2.3 Prepare today's students to thrive in an evolving technological landscape.

One of our authors, Sarah, was a member of a 2017 ISTE Technical Working Group, and recalls the conversation around developing the Educator Standards in the context of the Student Standards. These two sets of standards interplay to transform learning to prepare students for their future, as well as the present day. By nature of the Standards for Educators and for Students, educators have a common benchmark against which to measure their own progress and that of their students, which promotes digital equity for all.

ISTE Standards for Educators

Another of our authors, Nicol, participated in rounds of evaluations during the ISTE Standards for Educators refresh. Students in her masters in education course engaged in rounds of discussion about how each of the seven ISTE Standards for Educators (Figure 2.4) serves to enhance digital equity in some way. The goal of the Standards themselves is to provide transformational learning opportunities for each student around the world. Arguably, any efforts toward building educator efficacy contribute to solving inequities as they help to enhance learning opportunities for students. As ISTE stated,

> The ISTE Standards for Educators are your road map to helping students become empowered learners. These standards will deepen your practice, promote collaboration with peers, challenge you to rethink traditional approaches and prepare students to drive their own learning. (ISTE, 2017)

We will discuss the ISTE Standards for Coaches later in Chapter 3; for now, let's take a closer look at certain themes that emerged from all of the Standards. These three themes promote digital equity; interestingly (and perhaps subconsciously), the themes emerged in the following order: lifelong learning, communication, and transforming learning.

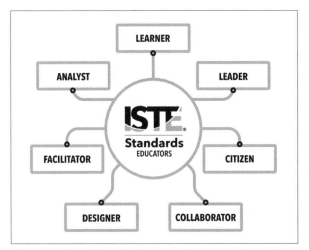

Figure 2.4 The ISTE Standards are an educator's road map for preparing today's students.

Lifelong Learning

Essentially, the goal of the first ISTE Standard for Educators, Learner, is to promote self-directed lifelong learning in order for learners to increase their capacity to deliver high-quality, transformational learning opportunities (ISTE, 2017). Much like the Empowered Learner from the Student Standards, educators are expected to set their own goals for learning, using the power of technology to enhance the experience (ISTE, 2016).

Think back to how you first became connected in your journey to professional learning. What was the spark? For many of us, it was through traditional face-to-face environments. A little over a decade ago, before the rise of social media, options for professional growth were limited, and educators were often at the mercy of whatever offerings were mandated to them. If they wanted choice over their learning to best support their students, their sole option was to connect during district professional development (PD) days or conferences.

Many conferences have a registration fee, therefore unless the school or district is willing to pay (and approve professional leave), this may present a barrier. As Sarah Thomas wrote,

> Creativity in schools should not be limited to the more affluent districts. All learners deserve high-quality teachers, who are motivated to grow professionally for the good of their students. (Thomas, 2017)

Additionally, such face-to-face events are usually held infrequently, and once sessions are over, attendees may not have support as they implement their new learning. However, we have come a long way in a very short time as we detailed in Chapters 2 and 3 of *Closing the Gap: Digital Equity Strategies for Teacher Prep Programs*, and now educators have a variety of options available.

Self-Directed Professional Learning

According to Dr. Randall Sampson, "Self-directed professional learning is what teachers want and need. Through self-directed professional development, teachers will be able to seamlessly reflect, align and implement best-practices; personalized growth is created and implemented by each teacher" (Sampson, 2015). Here are just a few ideas for teachers to take control of their professional learning journeys:

> **Twitter chats.** Twitter chats are "usually moderated and focused around a general topic. To filter all the chatter on Twitter into a single conversation a hashtag is used. A set time is also established so that the moderator...is available to engage in the conversation" (Cooper, 2013). These chats have proved invaluable to many educators around the world, and allow for multiple perspectives to be shared in a limited period of time. Furthermore, the conversation is then publicly archived on the hashtag itself. *You can find a list of Twitter chats at cybraryman.com/chats.html (Blumengarten, Hamilton, Murray, Evans, & Rochelle, n.d.).*

Voxer Groups. Voxer is what we call a freemium (free for the basics or pay for the premium) walkie-talkie application available on the web, iOS, and Android platforms. It allows large groups of up to 500 members to discuss topics and listen back asynchronously, facilitating global communication. *Although Voxer does not have the searchability of Twitter chats, you can find a crowdsourced list of groups at theedsquad.org/voxer (Corbell, Gauck, Pacheco, & Thomas, n.d.).*

Edcamps. Edcamp is a movement that began in 2010, which has expanded exponentially and globally. In essence, these events are spaces where educators come together for peer-to-peer learning. There are no presentations, only facilitated informal conversations; in fact, the daily schedule is decided by participants on the day of the event. While Edcamps are primarily based on geography, some online virtual Edcamps have emerged on platforms such as MIT Unhangout (unhangout.media.mit.edu) and even Voxer. *To find out more about Edcamp, please visit edcamp.org. For examples of virtual Edcamps, take a look at edcampedumatch.org and edcampvoice.com.*

Several other options exist on spaces such as Facebook, LinkedIn, YouTube, podcasting, and more. For anyone seeking to grow professionally, you have quite a selection!

Traditional PD Provides Benefits

Conferences and face-to-face meetups have benefits that the online world cannot replicate (and vice versa), and for many educators, they are an entry point into learning about more of the free and virtual options that can take their pedagogy to the next level. As the old saying goes, "you don't know what you don't know," and many of us have received our first exposure to the connected world by attending a conference.

According to research conducted Project Tomorrow (2018), conferences are still the second-most popular option for self-directed learning with 40% of respondents having reported being an attendee. This slightly trails watching videos online (46%) and is far more popular than social networking (33%) or engaging on Twitter (23%). Also apparent in Project Tomorrow's results is the rise in popularity of online self-directed learning, showing an increase in usage of social media since 2010. However, not a single category reported had adoption rates by the majority of respondents. Thus, although we have come a long way as a profession, we still have room to grow.

Communication

The second emergent theme from the Standards for Educators is that of communication. While the Standards for Students note the role of "Creative Communicator" (ISTE, 2016), there is no similarly worded standard in the Educator Standards. Instead, we see this theme referenced in standards such as Leader, Citizen, and Collaborator (ISTE, 2017). As Sarah Thomas explained,

> Many of the new Standards focus on transparency, with the aspiration of partnering with parents and community members. There is also an increased focus in acknowledging the voices of the most important stakeholders of all, the learners themselves. (Thomas, 2017)

The Leader standard is unique in two ways: It is not mirrored in the Standards for Students, and it is the only one that explicitly mentions equity, stating "advocate for equitable access to educational technology, digital content and learning opportunities to meet the diverse needs of all students" (Indicator B). However, as mentioned before, the Standards as a whole help support equity by providing a universal set of standards for educators to cultivate deep and active learning. Furthermore, the theme of equity is also heavily implied in Indicator A, "empowered learning with technology by engaging with education stakeholders," which suggests advocating for transformative learning experiences. This implication continues in Indicator C, "Model for colleagues the identification, exploration, evaluation, curation and adoption of new digital resources and tools for learning" (ISTE, 2017).

The Citizen standard (mirrored in the student standards as Digital Citizen) continues to gain importance, as it is easier than ever before to connect with other educators, schools, and stakeholders globally through social media. As Julia Freeland Fisher, director of education research at the Clayton Christensen Institute, pointed out,

> Social capital scholars have long pointed to the fact that opportunity flows through individuals' networks. In fact, according to some estimates, nearly 50 percent of jobs come through personal connections. In some cases, these come through strong ties, but they can also come through looser connections—what researchers call "weak ties"—which tend to offer up new information not necessarily contained in stronger-tie networks. (2018b)

The Organization for Economic Cooperation and Development (OECD) defines social capital as "networks together with shared norms, values and understandings that facilitate co-operation within or among groups," (Keeley, 2007, p. 103). OECD further delineates it into three categories:

Bonds: "links to...'people like us'... such as *family, close friends and people who share our culture or ethnicity*" (italics added for emphasis)

Bridges: "links that stretch beyond a shared sense of identity"

Linkages: "links to people or groups further up or lower down the social ladder" (Keeley, 2007, p. 103)

All students bring to the table with them some form of social capital; however, not all capital is held in equal regard in the eyes of society, as demonstrated by injustice, discrimination, and bias.

Some students might be fortunate to access bonds that will provide them with advantages established through family connections, culture, or even ethnicity. Other students who are members of groups that have been traditionally marginalized often find themselves pushed further to the sidelines. Through the power of social media, however, individuals are now beginning to disrupt this perpetual system of inequity. As Julia Freeland Fisher (2018a) argued, schools are in position to assist students in creating inclusive networks through bridges: "Schools looking to prepare students for the workforce and open doors for their students are pursuing models designed around the critical role that social capital plays in expanding access to opportunity." Likewise, schools can help prepare students through emerging technology platforms that cultivate relationships, both on and offline. To address this need, the Institute has created whoyouknow.org, which helps pair students "with coaches, experts, mentors, and peers—otherwise out of reach" (Christensen Institute, n.d.).

In an interview with Getting Smart (Ryerse & Berkeley, 2018), Fisher stated that schools can also help students access these bridge connections in the following ways:

- Focus on the network of care.

- See the school system in terms of "slots" in which a student can learn.

- Incorporate project-based learning.

- Expand students' access through advisory systems.

- Explore opportunities for change in school design.

Creative Communicators Transforming the World

Not only are educators in position to help students build networks—they can also support them in transforming the world. In Chapter 3 of *Closing the Gap: Digital Equity Strategies for Teacher Prep Programs*, we discussed how social media has played a significant role in today's society, as well as how it has impacted digital equity in that youth (and others) are now using various platforms, such as Twitter and YouTube, to advocate for themselves and organize at grassroots levels. We touched upon how movements that utilize hashtags have gained momentum through social networks. Another example of students using social media to positively impact the world is that of students at Marjory Stoneman Douglas High School in Parkland, Florida, who, after the shooting at their school, leveraged the power of social media to launch the Never Again movement and fight for change to prevent school shootings. As Sarah Stoeckl eloquently stated,

> When advocates of education technology talk about the ISTE Standards and digital tools used to change teaching and learning, we often give examples built within traditional subject areas and focused on feel-good activities by students. The "Never Again" students exhibit the ISTE Standards for Students in action, but in a way that reminds us we are not only preparing students for academic or career achievement, but also for life in a complicated, messy, often brutal world. (2018)

As more and more students begin to leverage social media for advocacy, educators must be prepared to support them in their acquisition of knowledge around digital citizenship without eliminating the platforms that allow students' voices to be heard (Howard, 2015). We view digital citizenship as a key component in the pursuit of digital equity. Promoting looking beyond traditional definitions of digital citizenship, where emphasis is placed on safety, and instead encouraging educators to look into more meaningful implications, Marie K. Heath stated,

The findings and discussion of this question suggest that uncritical usage of the term *digital citizenship* limits citizenship development in schools. Further, it hampers practitioners and scholars from imagining opportunities to use educational technology to develop pedagogies of engaged citizenship for social justice. These gaps lead to the fair critique of educational technology that technologists offer platitudes that technology can address issues of equity, but technologists have yet to develop strong pedagogies of liberation that leverage affordances of technology. (Heath, 2018, p. 5)

In her 2018 article, Heath identified three models of digital citizenship: *personally responsible citizen*, focusing on responsibility and character; *participatory citizen*, addressing organizing for social change; and *justice-oriented citizen*, using social media to "use technology to help interrogate established and oppressive norms" (p. 5). One key point identified regarding her study of justice-oriented citizenship models is that "several articles made general nods toward global citizenship or equity, often conflating access and equity or displaying a paternalistic and colonial attitude toward global citizenship" (p. 11), a sentiment echoed by Thomas (2018), who noted "... we tend to see a common theme: someone centering him/herself as the hero and saving the day, regardless of whether their 'saving' is welcomed and solicited, or not." This is an important, yet often overlooked, aspect to both digital citizenship and equity, as global communication and interaction is more available than ever before. We, as educators, need to model and embrace the entire continuum of digital citizenship in order to help our students navigate virtual spaces.

Digital Citizenship Resources

The need for good digital citizenship continues to grow as we move more of our interaction online. Furthermore, Howard (2015) said "as students grow older, they spend more time using digital devices and online networks. The use of these tools opens lines of communication globally, so now is the time more than ever to support our students." The following resources offer a few ways that you and your students can learn with the world.

DigCit Institute, DigCit Summit, DigCit Kids. "The Digital Citizenship Institute is an inclusive innovation network promoting a positive digital citizenship message of social good...[and provides] a community-driven approach to educating and empowering digital citizens to create solutions in local, global and digital communities" (DigCit Institute, n.d.). Founded and run by Dr. Marialice Curran, the DigCit Institute holds conferences around the world to help educate stakeholders on this crucial topic. Additionally, Dr. Curran's son, Curran Dee, is the Chief Kid Officer of DigCit Kids, which features "kids solving real problems in local, global & digital communities" (DigCit Kids, n.d.). *Find them at digcitinstitute.com, digcitinstitute.com/digcitsummit, and digcitkids.com.*

Our Global Classroom. Established by Bronwyn Joyce, Our Global Classroom is a "space to share ideas and thoughts with your learning community" using the FlipGrid platform. At the time of this writing, there have been over 200,000 views and 13,000 responses to various prompts from students around the world about real-world problems. Talk about authentic learning! *Find this project at flipgrid.com/whatif, using password "whatif."*

EduMatch. Founded by one of the authors in 2014, EduMatch is a global community of educators connecting and learning together, using various forms of social media. The organization has a global reach of over 30,000 educators, who come together on platforms such as Twitter, Voxer, Instagram, and others to discuss educational topics. EduMatch also hosts a podcast, which was featured by ISTE as one of the top podcasts of 2017; publishes crowdsourced and solo books; and, at the time of this writing, is preparing to launch a nonprofit arm to support grassroots projects of educators and students. *Find them at edumatch.org.*

Communication and Collaboration

Digital equity and digital citizenship go hand in hand. Students are increasingly utilizing their online networks, and as Collaborators, educators can use the power of their own networks to provide high-quality authentic learning experiences, to prepare students for an increasingly global world (ISTE Standards for Educators, 4: Collaborator, 2017). A key component of the Collaborator standard (paralleled in the Student Standards as Global Collaborator) focuses on transparency; engaging all stakeholders in the learning process. Collaboration as a form of communication tends to be overlooked, however, Collaborator calls it to the forefront. Within the standard, educators must communicate with colleagues, students, community members, and parents. Notably, Indicator D under the Collaborator standard speaks to the need to "demonstrate cultural competency when communicating with students, parents and colleagues and interact with them as co-collaborators in student learning." This brings to mind the notion of *culturally relevant, responsive,* and *sustaining* pedagogies, as explained in our first book (Howard et al., 2018). Digital equity cannot be separated from culturally relevant pedagogies. Doug Havard, a STEM Teacher on Special Assignment (TOSA) and Physics/Robotics Instructor from Southern California, agrees and recognizes the importance of building a social culture that is human-centered, rigorous, and includes place-based learning experiences for all students in the midst of digital equity challenges. He shares his thoughts in the "Culturally Responsive Computing" sidebar.

Educator Voices

Culturally Responsive Computing

By Doug Havard, STEM TOSA and Physics/Robotics Instructor

Not so long ago, pedagogical approaches to teaching and learning in our educational system were deeply contextualized by local living conditions and educative experiences: dominated by the interrelationships between the home, school, and community. Incongruencies on the means and ends of education, largely dominated by historical narratives and technological advancements throughout the mid-20th century, have led the school to become more institutionalized today (Greenwood, 2011). Along the way, accountability measures and standards-based teaching methods have attempted to stratify the educational ethos, a departure from the early form of education centered on experience (Spring, 2018). As a result of these standard-based approaches and the changing social and cultural nature of the American school, the emergent form of education over the last decade has led to a widening of the digital divide (van Dijk & Hacker, 2003). Contemporary research has revealed significant gaps in access, use, support networks, and skill in technoliteracies, particularly within underrepresented populations of students (Kahn & Kellner, 2005; Warschauer, Knobel, & Stone, 2004). In response to these philosophical stances, educational researchers have sought ways of bridging the access gap through *culturally responsive computing* (CRC) practices (Lachney, 2017; Lee, 2017; Scott, Sheridan, & Clark, 2015) and *place-based education* (Greenwood, 2011; Gruenewald, 2014) as counter-narrative pedagogical approaches which promote inclusion, digital equity, and self-efficacy.

Applying these perspectives, Scott and White (2013) sought to understand how unique STEM learning contexts employing CRC practices affected girls' pre- and post- programmatic engagement. Their research study, conducted on a sample of forty-one high school students participating in COMPUGIRLS, a National Science Foundation–sponsored program teaching technoliteracies to girls in digital media, game development, and virtual worlds, contended that girls are interested in technological fields despite a lack of culturally relevant opportunities to pursue such disciplines. They discovered the more complicated the technology and the higher the expectations, the more COMPUGIRLS participants expressed enjoyment. Moreover, Scott and White (2013) observed that the power of manipulation (e.g., to design and build an artifact that performs a task) not only intrigued participants, but also empowered them to perform individual research on specific technological topics in innovative ways—encouraging social change. This example of spiraling back to a time of connecting students, technology, and the world through educative experiences proposes an opportunity for reconnection between the means and ends of education today and our role as teacher educators.

My experiences as a K–12 STEM educator, STEM TOSA, and STEM program developer within a public high school have revealed the value and importance of building a social-culture that is human-centered, rigorous, place-based (has a positive role in the community), and connective to the discrete, individual experiences of students. These foci are not only reflected in the research presented above but emerged out of a number of experiences with my students while building a STEM-based program, namely through rigorous competition (e.g., US FIRST Robotics, NASA Student Launch, and Lemelson-MIT InvenTeam), but also through student-designed opportunities (TeenHacks Hackathon) and curricular endeavors (mechatronics colloquia) centered around instilling inventive practices through an interdisciplinary, human-centered engineering curriculum. The unstated challenge facing STEM educators in the K–12 setting is how to provide CRC experiences to students that afford access to computers with the ability to run industry-level software, an institutional knowledge base and practices to access technical content, financial support to enter into competitions and sustain future entries, and an equitable CRC curriculum to strengthen positive interactions between students' lives and technology. By maintaining a program focus on building community leaders, my colleagues and I centered our work around a methodology seeking to directly support and involve the community. The return on this place-based educational approach was a spiraling up of interconnected factors including opportunities for students to engage in solving problems in their community, technical experts reaching out in support of building an institutional knowledge-base, in-kind financial and material support from local industry, and a rise in program participation of our underrepresented female student population.

Matching curricular experiences which are culturally responsive and rigorous with community problem-solving has the opportunity to empower a generation of fledgling underrepresented scientists, technologists, engineers, and mathematicians. Although building social culture within your school and community can be initially slow, and often arduous, the power it places in the hands of students is transformative. Place-based educational practices which bridge the school and community will yield more real-world, problem-solving opportunities for students, access to digital resources, and supports for running difficult to maintain, albeit influential and inspiring, competitions such as US FIRST Robotics.

Transforming Learning

The final three standards, Designer, Facilitator, and Analyst, speak directly to the role of the teacher in the instructional process (ISTE, 2017). While the Designer standard speaks to the educator's ability to create learner-centric lessons, its counterpart in the ISTE Standards for Students (Innovative Designer) also deals with problem-solving and thinking outside the box (ISTE, 2016).

Facilitator speaks to the innovative learning environments and computational thinking as often seen in makerspaces, STEM/STEAM programs, and coding initiatives (see Computational Thinker and Knowledge Constructor in Standards for Students). Also overlapping with the aforementioned Student Standards is Analyst in the Standards for Educators, where data informs instruction to "support students in achieving their learning goals." Facilitator and Analyst intersect in that the former supports students in implementing a design process, while the latter has educators engaging in such a process themselves (ISTE, 2017). When considering these standards, it's important to keep in mind that

> Relevance and authenticity are two things that our learners crave. Many of our students aspire to create content, as opposed to passively consuming. Several ISTE standards promote student choice and voice in the classroom. (Thomas, 2017)

Models for Technology Integration

There are several popular models for technology integration that educators can use to self-evaluate where they stand, regarding their capacity to provide transformational learning opportunities for their students. Remember, not every lesson has to hit the highest levels of the rubric; instead, the goal is to build capacity so that each educator has the capability to reach the highest levels when appropriate. Simmons (in Thomas, 2017) wrote about three models in particular. Shown in Figure 2.5, the first model is SAMR.

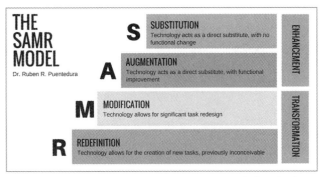

Figure 2.5 The SAMR model provides a practical guide for edtech integration. *(Image credit: Wikimedia Commons.)*

Originally developed by Dr. Ruben Puentedura, SAMR stands for substitution, augmentation, modification, and redefinition. You can learn more about SAMR at hippasus.com/rrpweblog.

Shown in Figure 2.6, the TPACK model focuses on technical knowledge, content knowledge, and pedagogical knowledge. These three forms of knowledge intersect in varying ways to create up to seven components. The highest level of mastery is TPACK, the sweet spot where each component intersects. If you're interested in learning more about this model, visit tpack.org.

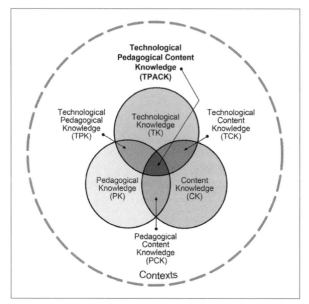

Figure 2.6 The TPACK model supports using digital tools for teaching and learning. *(Image credit: tpack.org.)*

The third model, Royce Kimmons' PIC-RAT (Figure 2.7) explores technology use and integration through the behaviors of both students and educators. On the student side, their relationship to technology may be passive, interactive, or creative, while educators may use the technology for replacement, amplification, or transformation. For more information on PIC-RAT, consult roycekimmons.com/tools/picrat.

Think about your last technology-infused lesson. Where does it stack up on each framework?

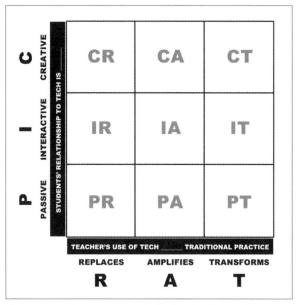

Figure 2.7 Evaluate your use of edtech using this matrix
(Image credit: roycekimmons.com.)

The ISTE Standards for Educators help promote equity by ensuring that each learner can receive access to high-quality teaching opportunities, regardless of their zip code. Cicely Day, an elementary teacher in Oakland Unified School District, understands the need for ensuring equity for her students and has faced her own challenges related to access. On a limited budget, Cicely has overcome barriers and continues to address digital inequities while making moves on a tight budget. She shares her story in the sidebar "Ballin' on a Budget."

Educator Voices

Ballin' on a Budget

by Cicely Day, Teacher, Data and Tech Lead

If you are reading this, you want to do all of the great things you see other schools and libraries doing with making and a makerspace, but may think you need a host of expensive tools, which are beyond your limited or nonexistent budget.

Well, let me tell you that you can have a makerspace in your classroom on a budget. There is no wrong or right way of making or even having a makerspace. The most important thing is to get started and try some things! Your makerspace can be in bags or tubs on your bookshelf. You can store things in your closet and take materials out when you need them. If you don't have space in your classroom, think about the hallway or a room that is not in use all of the time. A makerspace can be wherever you and a group are making. I started off with what I already had in my classroom: paint, crayons, markers, and paper. Cardboard will become your new best friend, so will felt and glue guns. My school had a treasure trove of construction paper, so I would think of projects I could use with that.

Now, I also have some Chromebooks, a Kindle, and an iPad. When Chromebooks were introduced at my school, however, we didn't have a class set, so I would set up four or five as a station for coding projects with Code.org and then later Scratch (scratch.mit.edu).

I started small and added things little by little. For example, I bought some inexpensive Ozobots (ozobot.com) to help my students learn about coding and have fun with robotics. Later, I added more programmable robots that would work with my Chromebooks and Kindle: a Sphero (sphero.com/education), a Dash, and a Dot (makewonder.com).

Many inexpensive options that work on a variety of devices are now available. Micro:bit (microbit.org), Makey-Makey (makeymakey.com), and Circuit Playground Express (adafruit.com) are great microcontrollers whose developers offer lots of support for students and teachers. If you are adventurous, you can get a Raspberry Pi (raspberrypi.org), which is also very affordable, if you have a monitor, keyboard, and mouse.

I am not saying that you have to buy all of your things like I did, but I am impatient and don't like waiting. If you can wait, plan out a budget, and think about the things you would like for your students to work on. Check to see if your colleagues have some of the things you are looking for. Share your resources with your colleagues. It helps expose more students to different materials and helps with your budget. Go to Michaels, Barnes & Noble, and JOANN, and sign up for their teacher discount programs, which help save you dollars when you are on a small budget. Sign up for DonorsChoose.org, and look for any organizations in your state and local area that offer matching funds programs. Some have a requirement for STEM/STEAM, math, or English language arts.

Having 3D printers, laser cutters, and other high-end equipment is nice, but that is not the only way to make or to have a makerspace. Thinking outside of the box, failing a bunch of times, and trying out different things will take you on a fun (and, at times, frustrating) journey. More importantly, it will help your students and you see how making can be a great way to think, create, heal, and build community.

DE Wisdom

A tasty cupcake and a sweet Twinkie are analogous to technology use and technology integration. Both are delicious and will serve a sweet tooth; however, the cream in the middle is the important part. The cream on the top of a cupcake can be easily removed without too much structural change to the dessert, much like what happens when technology is *used* in the classroom. If technology is simply used in the classroom—sometimes as an afterthought or quick addition to a lesson—it likely presents no structural change to a lesson. A Twinkie, on the other hand, has its cream in the center. If the cream were removed, the Twinkie would fall apart and make it difficult to eat. This is comparable to what we may observe when technology is *integrated* into a lesson. In the case of technology integration, technology serves a purpose that may not otherwise be realized if not integrated in a purposeful, impactful way into a lesson or activity. This simple use of technology makes building connections easy and is just a beginning to inciting students' curiosity and critical thinking.

— *Kim Roberson, Educator/Instructional Specialist
from Maryland*

Join the conversation on Twitter using #DigEquityBook, and share your analogies with us.

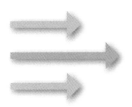

Chapter 3

WHAT DOES THIS MEAN FOR PROFESSIONAL LEARNING?

To close this divide, we must fully support educators with the skills and tools they need to power up the learning environment. While there are many ways that teachers develop their competencies, one research-backed strategy is classroom coaching.

—Cator, 2017

When teachers and coaches work side by side, the results are endless with regards to the innovative opportunities for educators and students. Similar to the team approach to solving a problem of practice discussed in Chapter 1, a collaborative effort to navigating new technologies maximizes the learning and output for all. We are encouraged by the pockets of inspiration and excellence where students and teachers are leveraging technology for collaboration, complex problem-solving, connecting across borders and boundaries, and engaging in innovative real-world projects. What all of these learning scenarios have in common is how they support the development of critical thinking skills and research skills while leaving room for creativity, problem-solving, and collaboration. Furthermore, such scenarios go beyond engaging students in their learning and support their development of a sense of agency for lifelong and life-wide learning (Cator, 2017). Knowing what we know, why not design all professional learning in such a way that supports this synergistic learning experience?

The Digital Promise Approach

Digital Promise is a nonprofit organization, formed by the United States Congress in 2008, with the mission "to accelerate innovation in education to improve opportunities to learn" (Digital Promise, n.d.). In 2018, the organization released a report from its Dynamic Learning Project (DLP), which examined technology coaching as a strategy to help teachers transform learning for students, focusing on promoting digital equity. As discussed in the previous chapter, professional learning (PL) opportunities are necessary to address the digital learning gap for educators and, thus, students.

For its Dynamic Learning Project, the organization sponsored a one-year grant for one full-time technology coach per campus in fifty schools across twenty districts. The project required four eight-week coaching sessions, where DLP coaches worked individually with teachers to help solve a technology challenge in their classrooms. The coaches received professional learning opportunities throughout the school year and were added to a community of other DLP coaches located across the country (Bakhshaei, M. et al., 2018, p. 11). Great attention was given to both the needs of the coaches and teachers overtime, which is a practice we should continue to adopt in efforts to achieve digital equity.

After the year-long project, 80% of participating teachers reported that they were now capable of using technology to provide students with transformative learning experiences. DLP Coaches also felt more confident in their coaching abilities. Digital Promise identified

> six core attributes of a strong coaching model, and five key qualities of a successful coach. The six core attributes are: partnerships, personalization, voluntary nature, situated in school/classroom, non-evaluative, and sustained. The five key qualities are: relationship builder, insider, strong communicator, tech believer, and experienced teacher. (Bakhshaei, M. et al., 2018, p. 5)

The DLP is clear proof of the benefits of ongoing coaching and professional learning.

PL Best Practices and Considerations

PL is the linchpin of any successful learning initiative, whether or not it involves technology. But when new technological tools are layered onto new learning initiatives, the need for training and support grows exponentially. Well-designed PL for technology-enhanced learning initiatives integrates tool training with content and pedagogy training. After all, if the intent in the classroom is to integrate technology with teaching and learning, then that integration must happen at the professional learning level as well.

Best practices for professional learning also include ongoing and embedded support. Effective educational leaders and coaches understand that one-off, standalone workshops do little to empower teachers to adopt new curriculum or instructional strategies. According to Yoon, Duncan, Lee, Scarloss, and Shapley (2007, in Vega, 2013), "when teachers receive well-designed professional development, an average of 49 hours spread over six to 12 months, they can increase student achievement by as much as 21 percentile points."

More than likely the development of a professional learning initiative occurs while your team is in the *planning for teaching and learning phase* of addressing a problem of practice, which supports the DLP findings that "relationship builder" and "strong communicator" are key qualities for a successful coach. Here are some helpful questions to discuss regarding your PL initiative:

- How does the PL plan specifically address the initiative's goals?

- How does the plan put teachers in the best possible position to actually use the technology?

- In what ways is the PL ongoing and/or job-embedded?

- How does the PL integrate the technology training with training on the learning initiative itself?

- How does the plan take into consideration the needs and profiles of adult learners, including the fact that all people, even adults, learn at different rates?

- Will teachers be able to get support when they need it? How?

- Does the professional development strategy scaffold the learning and make it possible for teachers to learn gradually?

- Do you see evidence that teachers will be able to learn the basics, apply them, and when ready, move on to instructional technologies and practices of greater complexity?

The ISTE Standards for Coaches can help with the development and facilitation of PL. Additionally, the Standards can serve as a yardstick by which to measure your PL/coaching efforts. We will now turn to an examination of how the Standards for Coaches further support digital equity.

PL versus PD

What, exactly, is the difference between professional learning and professional development (PD)? According to George Couros (2015),

- Professional development is something done to me, while professional learning is something I do for myself (which was reiterated by several people on Twitter).

- Professional development seems to be more connected to an "event" (conference) or an objective, where as professional learning is ongoing.

In this spirit, most of our discussions will use the term *PL*; however, the equally common term *PD* may occasionally appear interchangeably when we cite external resources.

▲ ▲ ▲

Supporting Coaches and Teachers

The ISTE Standards for Coaches (2011) are particularly relevant to digital equity in PL, as many professional learning opportunities are designed, organized, and facilitated by coaches. For the purposes of this discussion, we, like Future Ready (Dossin, n.d.), have consolidated many roles under the heading of coaches, including "instructional technology facilitators, instructional coaches, teachers on special assignment, curriculum and technology coordinators, lead teachers, and other educators who offer professional learning in schools and districts." Similar to other ISTE Standards, by their very nature the Standards for Coaches (Figure 3.1) promote digital equity by setting a common bar for which to aim; the end goal is for stakeholders in every role to facilitate transformational experiences that promote learning in authentic and relevant ways.

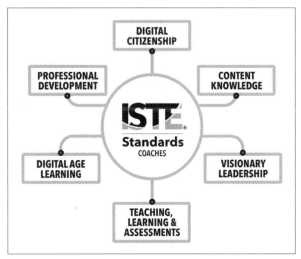

Figure 3.1 The ISTE Standards for Coaches intersect with the Educator and Student Standards in many ways.

These standards call for coaches "to promote excellence and support transformational change throughout the instructional environment" (ISTE, 2011). Coaches are key players in the transformational change process, because they typically have the knowledge and understanding of what it takes to be a teacher and a leader in these efforts. Coaches not only need to understand the needs of students, they also have to possess a keen ability to adjust their professional learning strategies to ensure they are meeting the needs of every teacher. Coaches are also consumed with thoughts on how to address the lingering issue of not having adequate time with educators who are in need of their support. For example, some teachers do not have access to substitute teachers and work with students after school, so they have limited time available to work with coaches during a regular school week.

Some coaches are faced with the challenge of supporting K–12 educators in their districts, and others seek to extend their efforts to address digital inequities beyond their district borders. In doing so, they encounter additional challenges with regards to educators' access to their PL. For example, a coach who facilitates PL outside of their district may charge a fee to offset the expense of holding such a session outside of regular school hours. Although this is an acceptable and understandable practice, it may prevent some educators from being able to attend certain PL opportunities.

One of the best ways to understand these challenges is to hear the stories of actual coaches. In "What are the Odds?" Abbey Futrell examines the difficulties of achieving a diverse audience for a professional learning provider, while in "It's All About the Mindset," you can read Carla Jefferson's story of how the right mindset helped propel her farming-community school district to transform learning while addressing digital equity challenges.

 Educator Voices

What Are the Odds?

by Abbey Futrell, Assistant Superintendent

In my many roles as a professional learning provider, I have provided professional development that was often free or provided through grants. Yet, specific populations of teachers consistently were not present and not included. Why? Was it lack of availability of substitute teachers? Was it lack of funding for hotels and travel? Was it lack of interest? Having attended and facilitated many other professional learning events and conferences, I noticed the lack of diversity, both in teacher attendance as well as facilitators of professional learning experiences for teachers. Again, why?

Together these trends point to a misconception that best practices related to learning for students don't apply to adults as learners. Research shows that students learn best from teachers who look like them. Research shows that students learn best when provided equitable learning opportunities. Research shows that equitable resources are essential for the optimal learning experience for students. Why would this same rationale not apply for our teachers?

The same inequities that exist for our students related to learning also exist for our teachers. In taking a deeper dive on a personal level to explore the reasons behind theses inequities, I learned:

- Some teachers can't get a substitute to attend professional learning sessions. Not because substitutes aren't available, but because these teachers are so good at handling "those" students, they can't be away from their classrooms.

- Funding is an issue. Although professional learning conferences are relatively affordable or even free, financial resources for registration costs, travel expenses, housing accommodations, and substitute wages are simply not available in some districts.

- The fact that students learn best from teachers who look like them is overlooked when offering professional learning opportunities for teachers.

- Students don't all learn the same way, but the aspect of personalization is forgotten when it comes to providing learning experiences for teachers.

The last two points are most troubling: Are we sending the message that there are no or few people of diverse backgrounds who are able to facilitate professional learning? Diversify those conference lineups!

Beating the Odds

According to Abbey, we must beat the odds when it comes to diversifying conference keynote and presenter lineups, which may in turn attract a more diverse teacher audience that mirrors today's student population. Why is diversifying PL spaces for educators an important digital equity topic to discuss? Abbey asserted,

> When we discuss equitable learning opportunities for students, those opportunities have to include our teachers. An equitable education means all students have access to teachers who are informed and prepared to facilitate exceptional learning experiences for teachers. A population of well-educated teachers is essential in creating a population of well-educated students.

Diverse learning spaces are essential for educators, as well as students, in efforts to achieve digital equity. The more diverse the learning space the greater the variance in the voices sharing and the higher the likelihood that you walk away from that learning experience with essential information to help you solve your own digital inequities. Learning from diverse groups of other educators fills in the gaps of knowledge for those educators who work in less diverse educational settings. Why would you need exposure to diverse learning spaces if you primarily teach one population of students? The answer is embedded in the question. A diverse learning space allows an opportunity to learn strategies that support all students. Rather than wait until there is a change in your student population to cram and struggle to create a sense of inclusivity for your own students, learn how to best support every learner and be ready to support any student.

There will clearly be moments when you cannot control a traditional PL environment. At the same time, we would be remiss if we didn't acknowledge that PL spaces are evolving. Despite their progress and potential, there is work to be done. We must continue to strive for inclusivity of diverse learners and cultural groups in PL learning spaces. Where can you begin?

Diversify your PLN. Reflect on who is in your PLN and ask, do I hear the same voice each time I seek support or look to collaborate on addressing digital inequities? If so, consider expanding your network to include the voices that are less familiar.

Recommend diverse speakers. Certain conferences, such as ISTE's Conference, seek suggestions for keynote speakers. Take advantage of these opportunities to recommend a diverse speaker who has a powerful story or message to share.

Try a new PL opportunity. We've already mentioned the broad range of digital inequities. Although your campus may be situated in an affluent community, consider attending a PL session focused on digital equity issues that differ from your own. Be open to learning the nuances of digital equity and how to serve a diverse population of students.

 Educator Voices

It's All About the Mindset

by Carla Jefferson, Instructional Technology Coordinator

The Darlington County School District (DCSD) school zone nestles right against the Great Pee River in rural South Carolina. Our "darling town" proudly hosts the annual NASCAR Bojangles Southern 500 race and the Sweet Potato Festival. Our primary source of income is farming. With a student population of approximately 10,500, our school district is 100% free/reduced lunch and 100% 1:1 with Apple devices. How do we do that, you ask? It's all about the mindset!

We believe in challenging our students and pushing their boundaries through classroom and life experiences, rigorous standards, and innovative teaching. Our district has embraced the concept of a 21st-century education. Creativity, collaboration, communication, critical thinking, and adaptability are key components in our classrooms as well as our day-to-day operations. Under the vision of our Executive Director Diane Sigmon, we were able to convince our school board and community that our students can compete in today's society given the proper tools and resources. Her favorite quote, "Why not Darlington?" resounded with all stakeholders and paved the path for our students. In 2015, our school board voted to fund this 2.5 million dollar initiative in perpetuity. After a three-year roll out process, all K–8 students are now 1:1 with iPad Airs and all Grade 9–12 students are 1:1 with MacBook Airs. High school students take their devices home. Each certified staff member is issued both a MacBook and an iPad.

Digital equity encompasses both access *and* opportunity, so our technology plan included a rigorous and in-depth professional development (PD) plan, as well. Our biggest challenge was not physical resources, but human ones. I am one of three district-level instructional technology coordinators that support more than 1,000 district staff members. We decided that the best way to get our teachers where they needed to be was through a variety of learning opportunities and activities that immersed them in unique learning experiences that could then transfer to our students. Here are some of the highlights:

> **iTEL (Interactive Technology for Every Learner).** In this 2010 pilot program, seventy-three teachers across twenty schools were given iPad carts to use in their classrooms. To gain a cart, teachers participated in two weeks of PD

through a district-designed, graduate-level course. Their building administrators participated in a one-week PD experience that focused on leadership in the digital age.

Essential knowledge proficiency. All certified staff in Darlington County are required to demonstrate basic knowledge in our three major tools: Apple devices, Google, and Schoology (our learning management system). Teachers can demonstrate their proficiency in a variety of ways: earning product certifications (Apple Teacher/Certified Google Educator), taking an opt-out assessment and completing performance tasks, or participating in a face-to-face course.

Train the trainers. Because of our limited human resources, we adopted a train-the-trainers model. Principals recommended teacher leaders from their schools to participate in various types of professional development. Train-the-trainer sessions are hosted for Apple devices, Google, and Schoology. In addition, we meet monthly with our yearly Digital Transformation Academy cohort.

Digital Transformation Academy. In this year-long professional development cohort, attendees have conversations not just about tools and resources, but also school culture and climate. They participate in challenge activities (Make a Spark!, BreakoutEDU, Build a Car, etc.), as well as work on educational certifications. For the past two years, 95% of the attendees have earned their Google Educator Level One (or Two) certification and are Apple Teachers. Teachers also work in collaborative groups to design content-appropriate lessons and PD resources so that they can go back to their schools and better support their teachers.

Digital Transformation Conference. Our annual conference has grown to 700 attendees and features sessions focusing on effective technology integration in the classroom. We stress focusing on the learning goal—not the tool. Presenters are encouraged to include the instructional skill in their session titles in an additional effort to shift the teacher mindset. Our 2018 conference hosted more than thirty concurrent sessions (95% of them led by our own teacher leaders) as well as a Conference Playground with activities revolving around student creation and critical thinking (green screens, robots, podcasting) and an Expert Lab, where attendees could work on information gained in an earlier session with support.

Global collaborations and activities. Through small incentives, teachers are encouraged to participate in collaborative and knowledge-sharing activities, such as The Global Read Aloud, Applied Digital Skills Week, Hour of Code, and Digital Learning Day. For example, my colleague Rhett Hughes and I host a weekly podcast at bit.ly/dcsdtransforms (#dcsdtransforms on Twitter), plus I share a monthly newsletter, Tech Tidbits, high-lighting tools, resources, and the amazing work of DCSD teachers. My colleague Hanna Hanlin sends out a monthly calendar, which focuses on an iPad app or tool and provides daily activities.

Technology portfolio. Last year, all certified staff made their first submissions to their digital portfolios: their best lesson of the year that incorporated the 4 Cs (Collaboration, Communication, Critical Thinking, and Creativity). Because it was our first year, we encouraged our hesitant teachers to ensure that one of the 4Cs was included. Each portfolio was reviewed by one of the three instructional technology coordinators, and we provided feedback on each. Even having spent all year with these teachers, we were completely blown away by what we saw: third graders making commercials that tied into social studies, sixth graders producing instructional math videos, middle school resource students making FlipGrid videos of student responses to text, kindergarteners creating ChatterPix videos of their favorite president, and self-contained special needs students creating presentations for their student-led IEP meetings!

Is what we do perfect? Nope. Do we get pushback? Sometimes. Although at times I feel we aren't moving fast enough, I am unbelievably proud of the work that we have done. Recently, I worked with fifth-grade students preparing for our annual Innovative Fair. They researched ecosystems, wrote a script, recorded themselves in front of a green screen, and turned the results into Auras. I was mostly a facilitator, someone they could talk through their issues with. And as I watched them, my heart almost burst with pride. It solidified my resolve. This—*they*—are why we continue to do this work.

Cultivating a Digital Equity Mindset for All

Carla offered excellent tips and strategies in "It's All About the Mindset." She and her team are great examples of what patience and collaboration can achieve in pursuit of digital equity. Perhaps you are seeking to shift the mindset on your own campus, and you're wondering what practical steps to take in this effort. Howard (2018) offered four tips to narrow the digital equity gap in teacher preparation that we find relevant for this conversation, so we have modified her four tips to help with your own efforts to cultivate a digital equity mindset on your campus:

Engage in honest conversations. Speaking openly and honestly about the digital inequities on your campus puts you one step closer to finding effective solutions. Remember when we encouraged you to collect data related to your problem of practice to analyze and utilize for planning teaching and learning? These conversations are extremely helpful, especially when they include authentic quantitative and qualitative data points. Quantitative data could include the percentage of students in your class and on your campus who have access to devices and the internet at home. Qualitative data might consist of the stories students share about the disparities in tech use between homes and classrooms. All of these data can be used to initiate an honest conversation with colleagues, administrators, parents, board members, and community stakeholders to determine the best solution for addressing your digital inequities. Anecdotal data about your personal frustrations with digital inequities are important, yet we encourage the inclusion of student data when approaching administrators about the challenges. Furthermore, we recommend approaching the honest conversation with a solution mindset to avoid the assumption that you're simply offering a list of complaints. If you're unsure about possible solutions, remember to connect with a colleague or a member of your PLN.

Support the shift in practice. Hopefully the ongoing honest conversations lead to a plan that actively addresses the digital inequities and a shift in practice. When the shift occurs, if you were one to spark the honest conversation, prepare to support the ongoing work to achieve digital equity. Again, when you don't have the immediate answer, look to your PLN and the stories of others. Remember that some parents will need more support than others with understanding the nuances related to digital equity. Additionally, parents may need ongoing support navigating any new devices or digital tools. Supporting parents with the shift in practice is an important step in the process of cultivating a digital equity mindset among all stakeholders.

Model innovation. Without question, you will model innovative uses of new technologies and digital tools for your students. Encourage this same practice amongst colleagues, perhaps during department or grade-level meetings. Multiple opportunities to engage in this form of informal PL give educators a chance to explore in a low-stakes environment where learning can occur through trial and error. Additionally, the culture of sharing encourages the cultivation of a digital equity mindset.

Re-evaluation through collaboration. Finally, remain open to re-evaluating your own technology practices and beliefs. As you collect data and have ongoing honest conversations with colleagues, collaboratively assess how you are addressing digital inequities. These re-evaluation meetings could also occur through informal PL, but either way they should inform any new shifts in your teaching and learning practice.

Innovative Professional Learning

In the first book of this series, we suggested that a wide array of professional learning communities exist at the very fingertips of teachers and coaches. Educators are overcoming the digital equity challenges related to access to professional learning (e.g., time constraints, limited funds, substitute teacher availability) by:

- Attending formal online professional learning events (e.g., conference livestreams)

- Building professional learning networks (PLN) in both face-to-face and online settings. According to Hodges, Carpenter, and Borthwick (2017), PLNs are an important element of professional development.

- Attending informal online professional learning opportunities (e.g., Voxer groups, Twitter Chats, Edcamps) absent of gatekeepers that often direct the learning

- Leveraging department meetings to include professional learning moments with peer educators

- Reading blogs and listening to podcasts to keep up with new advances in the field

Innovative professional learning opportunities should extend beyond the typical "click-and-get" sessions and one-hour sit-downs to include rich moments for gaining information, feedback, support, and kinship from one another. The goal should be to collectively become critical consumers of technologies to avoid the common pitfalls, such as chasing the hottest tools as opposed to the *most appropriate* tools for use, while addressing the most pressing digital equity concerns. According to findings from a study on teachers' professional learning preferences, teachers felt more supported in their work and better prepared to support their students' learning when they selected their own professional learning (PL) opportunities (Howard & Thomas, 2016). Out of the educators surveyed, 55.4% indicated that the PL sessions they were required to attend were not relevant to their work and 64% reported that these required PL sessions did not support their work. Roughly 98% of the educators surveyed indicated that they felt more supported and better prepared to support their students' learning when they self-selected their PL. What we know is that educators want what students want: choice and voice (Hertz, 2016).

DE Wisdom

School goes from a world of exploration to a minefield of frustrations. Being a teacher is not only about teaching content but also addressing that each student is on his or her own quest...walking into a classroom is either about exploration or survival. Some students come to school with extra provisions for the quest, while others just with the shirt on their back. Now, I not only see this with students, but I also see it with teachers who are overwhelmed by technology. When the teacher that has been teaching for years without technology is now thrust into a new world where every kid has a computer, does that feel like a child lost in translation?

— George Barcenas, Technology Coordinator

George's question is not uncommon and likely embodies exactly how some educators feel walking into a room filled with unfamiliar technologies they will soon use for teaching and learning. There are also educators who walk into such a room ready to explore and innovate, but they are unsure of how to effectively do so while supporting their own students with the acquisition of new tech skills. Do not be frightened by either challenge. Embrace the unknown and explore collaboratively with your peers and with your students. Yes, this may sound contradictory, especially when we are also saying that you should think about the learning goals before introducing a new tool. There is a tension that exists when you are seeking to explore and also trying to determine how, or if, your students will find a new tool useful in their learning. So first, do a bit of background investigation to ensure student's privacy and safety while assessing ease of use or access to "how-to" guides. Remember to observe your students closely as they explore, so you know when to step in and guide. Most importantly, don't forget that without moments of exploration you and your students potentially miss out on opportunities to access new digital tools, creating one of the very digital inequities you are seeking to eliminate.

Join the conversation on Twitter using #DigEquityBook, and tell us what you would do.

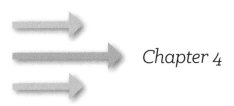

Chapter 4

WHAT'S NEXT FOR ACHIEVING DIGITAL EQUITY?

[School site principals] understand the critical connection of teacher effectiveness to educational equity, especially if their school is a Title I school or in an under-resourced community. Many principals as well as district administrators believe in the potential of technology to effectively level the playing field for all students, and increasingly they are putting those beliefs into action in their schools.

—Evans, 2018

So, where do we go from here? Research shows that schools and districts are making efforts to promote digital equity within their respective spheres of influence. According to a research briefing by Evans (2018) on data collected through Project Tomorrow, 60% of principals in the United States reported that their schools have a 1:1 policy in effect. Evans also shared that "43% of school site administrators state that the implementation of digital content is an effective tool for enabling equity ... [and]

report that instruction ... regularly includes the use of digital games, online textbooks and online videos, animations and simulations" (2018).

The target audience of the previous chapters may have appeared to be teachers and coaches; however, we recognize the overlap in efforts to achieve digital equity. Although this chapter may seem to be written for leaders, both teachers and coaches will find the information helpful in their own digital equity practices. As a point of clarification, we use the term *leaders* to indicate anyone who has power to influence the culture, policies, or climate of a school or district on a large scale. Therefore, *leaders* can be virtually any educational stakeholder, regardless of title. In "Journey Across the Digital Divide," Dr. Josue Falaise advises leaders at all levels on how to foster a digital age mindset. Meanwhile, later in this chapter we will discuss strategies for leaders, examining the recommendations of other organizations in this area: the Consortium for School Networking (CoSN) and the National Education Technology Plan (NETP).

 ## Educator Voices

Journey Across the Digital Divide

by Josue Falaise, Director of the Rutgers Institute for Improving Student Achievement

In the 2000–2001 school year, my last in the classroom, I was one of a handful of teachers that used an electronic grade book. In 2001–2002, my first as building leader and vice principal, the most sought-after devices were Blackberry cell phones and the HP Jornada PDA. In 2016–2017 as chief academic officer, I challenged myself to find creative ways to ensure all 11,000 students in the district had their own

Chromebook. Regardless of profession or role, every year we pursue new devices to keep up with the perceived 21st-century trends. Yet despite the changing trends in education technology, disparities between schools and districts remain, leading to a digital technology divide.

School leaders are challenged with decreasing budgets to purchase new devices and send teachers to edtech workshops to help build their knowledge base. District leaders struggle even more with budgetary obscurities, which impact their district's technology infrastructure, which trickles down to affect school leaders, classroom teachers, and ultimately students. As a leader of the Rutgers Institute for Improving Student Achievement (RIISA), a higher education professional development institute with the aim to support PK–12 school districts, I have challenged myself to design experiences that provide teachers and school and district leaders with edtech knowledge and insight that will directly and indirectly benefit students. Along my journey to this point, I have learned that the 21st-century school district, school, or classroom is not defined by tools and devices. It is a *mindset*.

Here are some ideas for each of you to help further that mindset in your district, school, and classroom:

District leaders. You can begin to identify edtech disparities or inequities that exist in your respective districts. Because districts vary in size, the capabilities to address concerns of infrastructure will also vary. Districts with more financial capital will be able to remedy infrastructure more expeditiously than districts with financial struggles. Therefore, seek to get the highest E-Rate discounts possible to help with infrastructure disparities. I suggest having a thorough dialogue with the community to consider movement towards a bring-your-own-device (BYOD) initiative. Many districts have seen significant benefits. However, the plan must include the purchase of devices for students whose families are unable pay for their personal devices. Find other district leaders within your county already hosting edtech workshops that could offer a number of workshop seats for your district's teachers to attend. Lastly, contact the Edcamp Foundation to assist with hosting a free district "unconference" with the theme of Edtech Equity. Then all participants attending will know to come prepared to discuss ideas, strategies, and practices around increasing equity with technology. (For more information on E-Rate discounts and the Schools and Libraries Universal Service Support Program, visit bit.ly/1quwIL6.)

School leaders. You can begin to model the integration of technology into everyday operations to get staff accustomed to sending and receiving communication via various apps like Google Sites, Google Drive, Google Sheets, and Google Forms, as well as social media platforms. If the number and percentage of parents, community members, and staff have declined reading your monthly newsletters, create social media accounts on various platforms for your entire school community to experience and highlight the activities and events daily. Utilize teachers with innovative skills of differentiation to train or coach their peers during the school day on integrating edtech into their lessons. If you have not already done so, you should create a

Twitter account and participate in some of the many group chats related to education and edtech. Model this expectation for your staff to help get them more involved on social media.

Classroom teachers. Begin connecting your students to sources outside of the classroom to observe and experience the content and concepts integrated with real-life activities. Despite an era of declining budgets, students can take virtual field trips via an app, observe doctors performing surgical procedures while communicating with viewers, or chat with NASA astronauts currently in space about geological, mathematical, and space science content. With minimal devices, students can rotate between stations and other planned activities. There could be design-thinking challenges in class requiring students to solve a real-world problem using everyday items found in their homes. Then they can articulate and possibly display how advancing technology can help their designed product solve their identified real-world problem.

Despite the challenges that may continue to exist due to the digital technology divide, RIISA seeks to begin decreasing the gap by hosting The Tech Equity Conference, enabling educators from around the world to meet with some of the edtech area experts in their field and grow their professional network. (For more information, see riisa.gse.rutgers.edu/init/tech-equity-conference.) Digital equity can be resolved by leaders of all levels ensuring that systems are established to address the needs of all students. It will be a long journey, but one we must travel when we truly believe that we exist to help all students learn and achieve.

Recommendations from CoSN

So far, much of our discussion has focused on what educators can do inside school walls to address digital equity, but the issue of equity affects our students at home just as much—and sometimes more. As the Consortium for School Networking (CoSN) explained,

> During the past two decades, efforts to provide America's schools with high speed Internet access have made great progress. Supported by the 2014 modernization of the federal government's E-Rate program and state funding efforts, a majority of schools now meet the FCC's short term connectivity goal of 100 Mbps/1000 students. However, the increasingly ubiquitous use of technology in instruction has resulted in a new digital divide between students who have home Internet access and those who do not. (CoSN, 2018)

As schools and districts are governmental organizations, we have a duty to provide equitable access to learning opportunities, including those required to be completed at home. In June 2018, CoSN released its Digital Equity Toolkit to combat the homework gap. Krueger (in McLaughlin, 2016) defined the homework gap as "the barriers students face when working on homework assignments without a reliable Internet source at home. This gap has widened as an increasing number of schools incorporate Internet-based learning into daily curriculum." Sprint, on its 1Million Project Foundation mission page, took a similar stance:

> 70% of America's school teachers assign homework to be completed online, but more than 5 million families with school-aged children do not have reliable internet connectivity at home. This disconnect leads to dramatically inequitable outcomes among our students. This

isn't fair. It isn't right. And it doesn't need to happen. (1Million Project Foundation, n.d.)

In its Toolkit, CoSN identified nine strategies leaders could explore to help promote digital equity. The first five are addressed to districts, and the last four target school leaders:

- Partner with community organizations to create homework hotspots.

- Promote low-cost broadband offerings.

- Deploy mobile hotspot programs.

- Install Wi-Fi on school buses.

- Build private LTE networks.

- Assemble a team and develop a shared vision.

- Assess existing community resources, gaps, and needs.

- Engage stakeholders and partners.

- Develop and execute a project plan.

We already addressed many of the latter points in Chapter 1 when discussing the process of addressing a problem of practice; therefore, the following sections will focus on the first five points.

Homework Hotspots

To support students without reliable home internet access, some school districts are joining with organizations and business in their communities to create "homework hotspots" that take advantage of existing Wi-Fi (CoSN, 2018). According to the 2015 CoSN Infrastructure Survey,

Fifteen percent of school systems report that there is community/business Wi-Fi available for students, a 50 percent increase from 2014. School costs tend to be minimal; partnerships can be branded to recognize businesses as partners in advancing digital equity and educational opportunity. (CoSN, 2018)

The CoSN Toolkit features several school districts that have mapped out such hotspots in the local community. For example, the Fairfax County Public School (VA) website states,

> Fairfax County Public Schools (FCPS) is pleased to provide you with an interactive map and a list of community Internet access sites in your neighborhood and the surrounding area. The list includes a variety of locations including libraries, and community, family, and other resource centers that are available for you and your student(s) to access the Internet and FCPS resources such as 24–7 Learning. (Fairfax County Public Schools, n.d.)

In addition to its community hotspot map, the district also offers many other initiatives such as: the option to check out devices and mobile hotspots from school libraries, computer donation intake, and computer clubhouses.

Community hotspots come with pros and cons. On one hand, students and families are welcome to go to participating businesses or organizations and utilize free Wi-Fi; on the other hand, there are also sometimes mitigating circumstances that prevent this from happening, such as transportation to the businesses. The more participating businesses and organizations offer this service, however, the more likely that students will be able to find access to high-speed internet close to home.

Low-Cost Broadband Offerings

According to the FCC, over half of rural Americans do not have access to high-speed internet access (Federal Communication Committee in DeGeurin, 2018). Poor urban areas are not faring much better, with sketchy tactics often being used to justify slower speeds in these areas (National Digital Inclusion Alliance in Bode, 2018). In the wake of government cuts to programs helping provide solutions (Larson, 2017), what can schools and districts do?

One of the initiatives mentioned in the CoSN Toolkit is EveryoneOn, which helps connect students and families to high-speed internet through partnerships with local internet service providers (ISPs). As the organization explained,

> EveryoneOn is a national nonprofit that creates social and economic opportunity by connecting everyone to the internet. Spurred by a challenge from the Federal Communications Commission to help connect all people in the United States, EveryoneOn began in 2012 as a public awareness campaign and digital inclusion pilot. Currently, we work to connect people living in the United States to low-cost home internet service, affordable computers and tablets, and digital literacy training. Since 2012, we have connected more than 600,000 people in 48 states, with the goal to connect one million people by 2020. (EveryoneOn, n.d.)

Besides low-cost connectivity solutions, ranging between $10 and $20 per month, EveryoneOn also features low-priced tablets and laptops, making the case that smartphones do not allow for screen-size-dependent activities, such as filling out job applications. While the organization focuses its initiatives mainly in California and on the East Coast of the United States, it provides services nationwide. To see a list of participating ISPs and criteria for selection, visit everyoneon.org/lowcost-offers.

Kajeet (2018) is a national organization that provides high-speed internet access outside of school to students and families through devices, such as SmartSpot and SmartBus. Additionally, the organization has worked to promote digital equity, having offered a grant in 2017, where five districts were awarded SmartBuses, hotspots, and cloud computing programs. Kajeet also offers resources on its site to help leaders secure funding to buy such tools and was a partner in creating the CoSN Digital Equity Toolkit.

Mobile Hotspots

CoSN recommends lending mobile hotspots as another alternative for after-school connectivity and asserted,

> Mobile hotspot lending programs can be an effective digital equity strategy, especially for students living in households that frequently move and for whom low-cost wired broadband plans may not be an effective solution. (CoSN, 2018)

CoSN further recommends that districts conduct a needs assessment to discover how to configure their hotspots. This assessment should include considerations surrounding the nature of the homework and the implications for data usage, access to streaming, and the type of filtering, if applicable. The Toolkit also mentions that any devices purchased by schools and districts receiving E-Rate funding must have CIPA [Children's Internet Protection Act]-compliant filtering.

Some organizations have programs that support mobile hotspots. One such initiative is the 1Million Project through Sprint. Its mission is "to help 1 million high school students who do not have reliable Internet access at home reach their full potential by giving them mobile devices and free high-speed Internet access" (1Million Project Foundation, n.d.). In its first year of implementation, the program donated 113,000 devices to more than 1,400 high schools in 120 districts across 31 states. Within this program, eligible high school students receive:

- 3 GB per month of free high-speed LTE data while on the Sprint Network

- A free smartphone, tablet, or hotspot device

- Free Sprint wireless service for up to four years

Interested schools and districts can find out more and apply at 1millionproject.org/schools.

Similarly, the EmpowerED program through T-Mobile provides devices and mobile service to schools receiving Title I funding, with at least 40% of students receiving free and reduced meals services. Unlike the 1Million Project, this program is open to students in Grades K-12, including private and charter schools. Successful applicants enter a two-year contract and are accepted on an ongoing basis. This program also includes a professional development program for educators on how to leverage the devices (T-Mobile, n.d.). Find out more at uncarrier.t-mobile.com/empowered.

School Bus Wi-Fi

Without a reliable internet connection at home, digital age homework can be a challenge:

> Teachers expect that students can do their homework from home, which requires Internet. While many low-income students [in the United States] have a phone, it typically is on a data plan. Imagine trying to write your senior thesis or apply for college on a smartphone using Wi-Fi at a McDonald's. (Krueger in Randhawa, 2017)

As a third strategy to increase internet access, some districts have begun equipping their school buses with Wi-Fi, allowing students to complete their homework on their rides to and from schools. Technology giant Google for Education (n.d.) has partnered with CoSN and Kajeet to sponsor "rolling study halls."

This initiative mainly focuses its efforts on rural districts where infrastructure remains a major challenge for many families and even schools. Often, students experience long bus rides to and from school, as well as unavailability of high-speed internet access at home. As stated by Kinch (2018), "many American children from rural areas have to ride the bus for 1–2 hours a day just to get to and from school. Traditionally, this time has been used for gossip and naps. Now, it can be used for something more productive: Homework."

The program focuses on three main goals: expanding access, expanding support, and expanding in the community. All buses are powered by the Kajeet SmartBus, and the initiative spanned twelve states in the 2017–18 school year (Kajeet, 2018). Michael Flood, Vice President of Strategy, shared that the company uses robust antennae on the buses, which can also send an enhanced signal to remote areas (in Schlosser, 2017).

Some schools and districts have decided to take action on their own. In 2011, former Coachella Valley Unified School District Superintendent Darryl Adams spearheaded an initiative to increase access to technology and high-speed internet access in his district:

> We have 1,250 square miles to cover, larger than the state of Rhode Island. So, when we found out there were spots in areas where students were not connected, we said, well, how can we get them connected? And so one of the ways was, we said, "look, we've got 100 buses. Let's put Wi-Fi routers on those buses. And let's park them where the need is." (Adams in Nazar, 2016)

The district passed a $45 million program dubbed Wi-Fi on Wheels, powered by solar panels. Additionally, buses were parked in neighborhoods overnight, providing hotspot access with a 150-foot radius to provide access to community members.

Huntsville City School began to equip buses with hotspots in school year 2015–16, and reported an additional benefit of a drop in discipline incidents (Huggins, 2015).

Currently, there is legislation pending in Congress to allow school bus Wi-Fi to be bought with E-Rate funding (Udall, 2018). Collectively, the nation holds its breath as we wait to see what will come as a result.

Private LTE Networks

One newer, more outside-of-the-box solution is for districts to build their own private LTE networks to provide home connectivity. As CoSN explained,

> Building private LTE networks is one of the most ambitious and innovative digital equity approaches. One way in which districts are doing this is by repurposing Educational Broadband Service (EBS) spectrum. EBS spectrum is a locally licensed prime mobile spectrum band in the 2.5 GHz frequency range used for advanced 4G wireless service. For additional background and technical information, visit EBSspectrum.org. (CoSN, 2018)

Albemarle School District in Virginia is a district with both urban and rural areas, the latter of which is widely located in mountainous regions where access to phone and cable high-speed internet is slow. Therefore, the district, in partnership with the FCC's Educational Broadband Service (EBS), mounted robust antennae atop school buildings. These antennae had a range of an eight-mile radius, and were connected through the fiber network used by the school (Siefer, 2015). As Vince Scheivert, Chief Information Officer of Albemarle County Public Schools, explained,

> We in Albemarle County Public Schools view technology as a force multiplier—it's an enabler that accelerates and

broadens the achievement potential of all students. Our vision is to build services that provide 15,000 users across 30 campuses with the latest resources and capabilities they need to be successful, lifelong learners. We are very proud of our most recent project to construct a county-wide LTE network that will bring broadband access to all students within Albemarle County's 726 square miles. We see this as a game changer not only for our students but for our community. (In Landers, 2015)

 Educator Voices

Engaging Students in Entrepreneurship

by Chris Aviles, Education Technology Coach

Like most businesses, my first Education Corporation (EdCorp), FH Gizmos, was born out of the need to solve a problem. At Knollwood Middle School in Fair Haven, New Jersey, I created a makerspace and STEAM class, called The Innovation Lab, for fifth and sixth graders to practice design thinking and to make for others. My goal was to expose my students to computer science, engineering, and the digital arts through project-based learning (PBL) and, more importantly, to develop the soft skills they'd need to be successful adults. Six months after launching The Innovation Lab, I realized I had a problem.

One way I exposed students to engineering was by having them take apart, analyze, and reassemble unwanted electronics donated by our community. Students love to deconstruct these electronics, see how they work, and then try to reassemble them. The reassembly part usually didn't go so well. Students often struggled to put the electronics back together. I had full-sized garbage cans of parts piling up in the lab—that was a problem. To put a dent in the waste we were generating, I created the Parts to Arts project. After taking something apart, if students couldn't put it back together, they were challenged to upcycle the parts into pieces of art. Like deconstructing the electronics, my kids loved the Parts to Arts initiative. They were producing tons of art—but now that was piling up.

A Student Solution

Listening to student voices and letting my students have ownership of their classroom is important to me, so I presented the problem as a design challenge to them: What can we do with these Part to Arts projects piling up besides throw them away? After some brainstorming and collaboration, the students' voice was unanimous: Sell it. I built an online marketplace for them with Wordpress, and every student team got a login to the site to create their own product pages. After reviewing and approving each, I linked them to the homepage. When customers visited the homepage they would be able to see all of the products students had for sale.

What happened next was like nothing I've ever experienced in education: My kids went nuts. Students not only put their Parts to Arts projects up for sale, but they also started to offer all kinds of different products. Students were selling items such as 3D designs, custom YouTube Artwork, Minecraft skins, and school supplies. One team was even selling custom theme songs. Students began to form teams around ideas they had for products they could sell. As they worked together to create art or build products, they began to talk about their teams, ideas, and products as if they were running a real business together.

I told students if we were going to make any sales, we had to buy a domain. To buy a domain, we needed a name. I had them research what makes a good business name and encouraged them to come up with a name that would be special to their school. After a lot of workshopping, we came up with FH Gizmos. FH for Fair Haven, and Gizmos because it was vague enough that they could sell anything they wanted on the marketplace, not just upcycled art projects. From there, students developed a mission statement, slogan, and logo. Together we filled the FH Gizmos homepage with content and branding. Students created advertising for FH Gizmos as well as their own individual businesses. Our principal, Cheryl Cuddihy, gave students a $75 loan and an Oriental Trading catalog to get the pop-up store off the ground. Students ordered inventory, decorated a cart, and hung up flyers announcing the creation of the FH Gizmos pop-up shop. We were ready to go to market: In January of 2016, FH Gizmos launched.

The Next Phase

To share the awesome FH Gizmos-entrepreneurship experience, I wrote an article for *EdSurge*, a popular edtech blog. Little did I realize that Real World Scholars (RWS) would read it and reach out to me with an amazing opportunity: an inventory grant that would help turn FH Gizmos into a real student-run startup. RWS (realworldscholars.org) provides funding for K–12 teachers to build student-run Education Corporations (EdCorps) in their classrooms because they believe teaching through entrepreneurship makes student learning real and relevant.

Funding in hand, we started the next school year by reimagining FH Gizmos. If it could be anything, what would we want FH Gizmos to be? We decided that we wanted to use design thinking in our school and community to find and solve problems. If we believed that the solution to that problem could help others, we would sell it. We also decided that FH Gizmos was a social business, so we started our own charity called FH Gives. Students voted to give 25% of our profit to FH Gives and use this money to do good in our community—our slogan: Your problem is our project!

We spent six months interviewing users to help students gain empathy for their needs, brainstorming and prototyping possible solutions, and testing solutions with users who shared the same problem. We found a lot of problems that needed solving and even managed to solve quiet a few of them. When we failed to solve a problem, students were still learning, and I was excited to see them begin to reframe failure as iteration.

Serious, Deep Learning

Teaching through entrepreneurship has been the most rewarding experience of my teaching career. In all of the success we've had and even in all of the failures, there has been significant learning happening all along the way. Entrepreneurship has motivated my students because they see what they're learning has real-world applications; they are applying it as they're learning it! Students come up with the driving questions they want to answer, because they need that knowledge to help their businesses grow. Students are learning math, art, science, English—everything that we traditionally teach in silos for some weird reason—in an authentic way. Students are no longer consumers in my class, they're creators and producers. As they do their products, students are shipping their thoughts and ideas all over the world. Thanks to entrepreneurship, students have rushed right past engagement to empowerment. There is no better vehicle for creating the experiences that our kids need to stretch themselves and harden the skills and growth mindset it takes to be successful not just in school or business, but in life too, than entrepreneurship.

Reach Out and Try

Now, if you look up the Fair Haven school district, you'll see that we are an affluent school district. Did our privilege make our program possible? True, my kids have access to much that others don't. When the program launched two years ago, however, I took *no budget* from my school. I'm not just in this to make learning better for my kids. I want to make learning better for *all* kids. After running this program on a $0 budget, I am confident any school can do it. Like I tell my kids, it comes down to hustle and heart.

By putting our work out into the real world and using social media to amplify our voice, we were able to land support from the Real World Scholars charity and Slack as our first client. If you have a phone, you can run a successful marketing campaign from the classroom. By sharing the great things students have done, you create the opportunity for someone to want to invest in your class.

Additional Recommendations from NETP

The National Education Technology Plan, or NETP (U.S. Department of Education, Office of Educational Technology, 2017) warns against the "missed opportunity" (p. 12) to connect students and families, as access to learning can and should continue outside the four walls of the school building. The report pointed to online and blended learning as examples of how this might occur and stated,

> Schools and districts that are deciding how to incor-
> porate educational technology in student learning
> should actively involve and engage families during early
> development and implementation of their digital trans-
> formation. (p. 11)

In Section 3, Leadership, NETP recommends that schools
and districts look to leverage Student Support and Academic
Enrichment (SSAE) Grants. One focus area of these grants is to
support the effective use of technology, namely in "rural, remote
and underserved areas" (p. 50).

One important thing for leaders to keep in mind regarding technology initiatives is sustainability. NETP recommended:

> Technology investments are not onetime [sic] expenses.
> Although one-time grants and other supplemental
> funding sources can serve as catalysts for establishing
> technology in learning efforts, they are not sustainable as
> schools and districts build toward a long-term vision and
> plan. When devices reach the end of life and infrastruc-
> ture equipment becomes obsolete, districts and schools
> should have a reliable means to replace or upgrade
> them. Leaders should consider technology an ongoing,
> line-item expense from the very beginning of planning
> technology implementation. (p. 52)

One Final Note

In this chapter, we have examined several solutions for leaders
to help promote digital equity in their school and districts,
including hotspots, connecting families to low-cost broadband,
and building private networks. At this time, we would also like
to differentiate between two commonly used terms: *top-down*
and *grassroots*. Top-down initiatives are typically suggested or

mandated by an individual or department of high-rank (i.e. Superintendent, Board of Education) when looking at education from a traditional lens. Most of our solutions presented within this chapter fit this paradigm.

On the other hand, grassroots initiatives generally start with a single individual or group, and momentum typically gathers through word of mouth until the change eventually becomes part of the culture. Grassroots initiatives are also important in the digital equity process. These movements can involve supporters from any role, but the process tends to move more slowly as these generally are not mandated. It's interesting to see what happens over time, as initiators of successful grassroots movements sometimes eventually find themselves in positions to create top-down initiatives. If anything, this underscores the need to remain committed to lifelong learning, as described in Chapter 2.

DE Wisdom

There is a great need for our digital equity conversations to begin shifting some of the attention from access onto quality and effective use of instructional tools. When the term *digital equity* comes up in conversations with executive leadership, far too often, the focus is access. The questions posed become *'how do we get more devices?'* or *'when will our schools be 1:1?'* In considering the move to 1:1, it is important to keep in mind that it's not just about students having access to devices. Because *all* students have the right to a good education, the questions that need to be addressed and monitored should be along the lines of: *what are our students being asked to do with the devices; does the activity help prepare for graduation, college, or career?* Technology, used effectively, can assist in providing invaluable learning opportunities to students, who in many circumstances, would never have received exposure or experienced.

To truly prepare our students for college and careers, an expectation of using technology for delivering instruction along with a shift in how teachers teach integrating technology must occur. All must be ready, willing, and able to move from a teacher-centered to student-centered classroom teaching environment, and employ personalized learning where students take ownership and actively participate in the creation of their learning and acquire and build on skills needed to be successful in the workforce.

Some of our teachers have made the shift by adopting a personalized learning practice. However, we still have a large number who remain the sole drivers in the delivery of curriculum. Students need to be able to communicate, be creative in their approach to problem-solving, analyze, understand how to find and utilize information.

— *Dr. Lisa Spencer, Director of Instructional Technology and Support*

Educational leaders and coaches work hand in hand with teachers to prepare students for graduation, college, and future careers. Together they *identify, analyze,* and *plan for teaching and learning around* their own district's problem of practice related to digital equity. In some instances, the problem of practice may simply be that there are limited numbers of devices on a school campus. As leaders make decisions to move to 1:1, or continue strengthening current programs, we must remember the significance of *planning for teaching and learning*. Dr. Spencer encourages leaders to do just that: to look beyond the ongoing line-item expense of technology and to think more deeply about whether we are asking students to use the technology they now have access to effectively.

Dr. Spencer acknowledges that a shift must occur in how teachers support students. Whether laying the foundation for employing the initiatives that Dr. Spencer mentions (e.g., personalized learning) or supporting the ones mentioned earlier in this chapter (e.g., grassroots movements), we also recognize the need for a shift in how leaders support teachers in addition to students. Howard and Howard (2017) asserted that teachers and students are generally positive about adopting new technologies when supported by leaders and given choice about their learning. The opportunity for teachers and students to express what they need further ensures a positive environment in which everyone drives their own personal learning.

CONCLUSION

Over the years, the naming conventions of the various ISTE Standards have changed to follow the trends of the field. We have seen the same with regards to the use of terms such as *digital divide* and *digital equity.* No matter what term we use, we agree with Susan Bearden, Chief Innovation Officer at CoSN, that "there is no silver bullet for addressing digital equity in school communities" (Belastock, 2018). As we continue to think about the most effective and efficient ways to support all learners, we suggest the goal should be for all educators to understand the nuances of each set of ISTE Standards to best address digital inequities and prepare for future changes in the K–12 classroom.

We realize that supporting teachers for utilizing emerging technologies in their K–12 classrooms has its challenges for coaches. We also recognize that without teachers and coaches working on the same team to address digital equity issues, solving the current problems will never take priority. Research and stories discussed throughout this book indicate that teachers, coaches, and leaders can make a huge impact on learning for students.

In our first book, we proposed that now is the time for university professors to be learners alongside their students (preservice teachers) in order to be best prepared to take on the work of achieving digital equity. The collaborative work cannot stop in teacher education as multiple perspectives are an essential component to achieving sustainable results when solving a problem of practice. Coaches, leaders, and teachers bringing their knowledge together makes for a more robust approach to transforming learning for students. We'd even go as far as saying that students should also be included in this process.

Krueger and James (2017) suggested the right to digital equity ensures the right to connect to needed resources—anywhere, anytime. We believe this statement not only applies to K–12 students, but also educators as they are faced with their own digital inequities. Clearly, the work is never-ending and cyclical as technology will continue to evolve, but now is the time for leveling up efforts to closing the digital equity gap.

We'd like to offer one final takeaway in Table C.1, which you may wish to consider using as you practice digital equity. You might use it as-is or as a guide when analyzing your problem of practice before developing your plan for teaching and learning.

Table C.1 Digital Equity versus Digital Inequity in K–12 Classrooms

Digital Equity	Digital Inequity
Educators selecting the tech tools based upon pedagogical needs while considering the access, privacy, safety, and ease of use for students	Educators choosing a tool only because it is popular, forgetting to connect it to learning
Educators engaging in active and collaborative learning as they determine the best digital equity strategies for their own classrooms	Allowing opportunities for collaborative learning with new technologies for K–12 students only, with no time given for educators to explore
Connecting with other educators globally to learn together and potentially plan for classroom collaborations based on mutual teaching and learning goals	Connecting with other K–12 classes globally to "teach" them without also learning from (and with) them
Ensuring a tool is culturally appropriate and inclusive of non-offensive imagery and current language (e.g., refers to enslaved peoples instead of slaves)	Using a tool regardless of harmful language and offensive imagery
Assessing the numbers of devices in your class to determine effective grouping strategies (e.g. 3:1 or 4:1)	Allowing only students who "finish" their work to use technology
Flipping instruction for K–12 students, but also making sure there are opportunities for students to use the technology in the classroom in the event they do not have Wi-Fi access at home	Assigning digital homework without first assessing the access to devices and adequate connectivity at home

REFERENCES

1Million Project Foundation. (n.d.). *1Million Project*. Retrieved from www.1millionproject.org

1Million Project Foundation. (n.d.). *Potential is everywhere. Opportunity is not*. Retrieved from www.1millionproject.org/our-mission

Bakhshaei, M., Hardy, A., Francisco, A., Noakes, S., & Fusco, J. (2018). Fostering powerful use of technology through instructional coaching: Results from the pilot year of the Dynamic Learning Project. *Digital Promise*. Retrieved from https://digitalpromise.org/wp-content/uploads/2018/08/DLP_CoachingReport_2018.pdf

Belastock, E. (2018, September 27.) Three digital equity leaders call to action for students without home Internet access Blog post]. *T&L Advisor Blog*. Retrieved from https://www.techlearning.com/tl-advisor-blog/digital-equity-leaders-call-action-students-without-home-internet-access

Blumengarten, J., Hamilton, C., Murray, T., Evans, C., & Rochelle, J. (n.d.). *About—Education chats*. Retrieved from https://sites.google.com/site/twittereducationchats/home

Bode, K. (2018, September 24). How bad maps are ruining American broadband. *The Verge*. Retrieved from https://www.theverge.com/2018/9/24/17882842/us-internet-broadband-map-isp-fcc-wireless-competition

Boser, U. (2013, June 14). Are schools getting a big enough bang for their education technology buck? *Center for American Progress*. Retrieved from https://www.americanprogress.org/issues/education/ reports/2013/06/14/66485/are-schools-getting-a-big-enough-bang-for-their-education-technology-buck

Cassel, R. N., & Kolstad, R. (1998). The critical job-skills requirements for the 21st century: Living and working with people. *Journal of Instructional Psychology, 25*(3), 176–180.

Cator, K. (2017, July 26). Addressing the digital learning gap with effective educator coaching [Blog post]. Retrieved from https://digitalpromise.org/2017/07/26/addressing-the-digital-learning-gap-with-effective-educator-coaching

Christensen Institute. (n.d.). *Who you know matters.* Retrieved from https://whoyouknow.org

Cooper, S. (2013, September 30). The ultimate guide to hosting a tweet chat. *Forbes.* Retrieved from https://www.forbes.com/sites/stevecooper/2013/09/30/the-ultimate-guide-to-hosting-a-tweet-chat/#6e4a441231ee

Corbell, K., Gauck, H., Pacheco, A., & Thomas, S. (n.d.). List of Voxer groups. *The EdSquad.* Retrieved from www.theedsquad.org/voxer

Cortez, M. B. (2017, April 17). Q&A: Richard Culatta aims to use government experience as new ISTE CEO. *Edtech.* Retrieved from https://edtechmagazine.com/k12/article/2017/04/qa-richard-culatta-aims-use-government-experience-new-iste-ceo

CoSN. (2018). *Digital equity toolkit.* Retrieved from https://cosn.org/digitalequity

Couros, G. (2015, November 12). Professional development and professional learning #miamidevice [Blog post]. Retrieved from https://georgecouros.ca/blog/archives/5791

Davis, T., Fuller, M., Jackson, S., Pittman, J., & Sweet, J. (2007). *A national consideration of digital equity.* Washington, DC: International Society for Technology in Education (ISTE).

DeGeurin, M. (2018, September 12). How new FCC rollbacks could cut off rural Americans from the Internet. *Intelligencer.* Retrieved from nymag.com/intelligencer/2018/09/fcc-lifeline-rollback-cut-internet-access-to-rural-america.html

DigCit Institute. (n.d.). *Home.* Retrieved from digcitinstitute.com

DigCit Kids. (n.d.). *DigCit Kids.* Retrieved from www.digcitkids.com

Digital Promise. (n.d.). *About.* Retrieved from https://digitalpromise.org/about

Dossin, L. (n.d.). *Future Ready Frameworks.* Retrieved from https://futureready.org/about-the-effort/framework

Evans, J. A. (2018). The educational equity imperative: Leveraging technology to empower learning for all. *Speak Up.* Retrieved from https://tomorrow.org/speakup/speakup2017-educational-equity-imperative-september2018.html

EveryoneOn. (n.d.). *About us.* Retrieved from https://www.everyoneon.org/about-us-the-digital-divide

Fairfax County Public Schools. (n.d.). *Community Internet access map.* Retrieved from https://www.fcps.edu/resources/technology/community-internet-access-map

Fisher, J. F. (2018, September 28). Getting Smart: Why youth need social capital. *Christensen Institute.* Retrieved from https://www.christenseninstitute.org/podcast/getting-smart-why-youth-need-social-capital

Fisher, J. F. (2018, October 12). Why a web of connections—not a single relationship—should surround students. Christensen Institute. Retrieved from https://www.christenseninstitute.org/blog/webofconnections

Google for Education. (n.d.). *Rolling study halls.* Retrieved from https://edu.google.com/giving/rolling-study-halls/?modal_active=none

Greenwood, D. A. (2011). Why place matters: Environment, culture, and education. In Tozer, S., Gallegos, B., et al. (Eds.), *Handbook of research in the social foundations of education* (pp. 632–640). New York: Routledge.

Gruenewald, D. A. (2014). Place-based education: Grounding culturally responsive teaching in geographical diversity. In *Place-based education in the global age* (pp. 161–178). New York: Routledge.

Heath, M. K. (2018). What kind of (digital) citizen? A between-studies analysis of research and teaching for democracy. *International Journal of Information and Learning Technology. 35*(5), 342–356.

Hertz, M. B. (2016, April 15). Why Edcamp is the future of PD [Blog post]. *Edutopia: A George Lucas Educational Foundation.* Retrieved from https://www.edutopia.org/blog/edcamp-is-future-of-pd-mary-beth-hertz

Hiefield, M., & Carter, N. (2018, October 3). *There's more to digital equity than devices and bandwidth.* Retrieved from https://www.iste.org/explore/articleDetail?articleid=2279

Hiefield, M., & Monterosa, V. (2018, October 16). We're closing the digital divide. Now let's end the participation gap. *EdSurge.* Retrieved from https://www.edsurge.com/news/2018-10-16-we-re-closing-the-digital-divide-now-let-s-end-the-participation-gap

Hodges, C. B., Carpenter, J. P., & Borthwick, A. C. (2017). Commentary: Response of the American Association of Colleges for Teacher Education to "An interview with Joseph South" regarding the preparation of educators to evaluate the efficacy of educational technology. *Contemporary Issues in Technology and Teacher Education, 17*(1), 17–23.

Howard, N. R. (2015, April 27). Cyber safety: Mock it, don't block it [Blog post]. *Edutopia: A George Lucas Educational Foundation*. Retrieved from https://www.edutopia.org/discussion/cybersafety-mock-it-dont-block-it

Howard, N. R. (2018, September 21). 4 strategies to narrow the digital equity gap for preservice teachers [Blog post]. *ISTE*. Retrieved from https://www.iste.org/explore/articleDetail?articleid=2278

Howard, N. R., & Howard, K. E. (2017). Using tablet technologies to engage and motivate urban high school students. *International Journal of Educational Technology, 4*(2), 66–74.

Howard, N. R., & Thomas, S. J. (2016, July 20). Edcamps: The new professional development [Blog post]. *Edutopia: A George Lucas Educational Foundation*. Retrieved from https://www.edutopia.org/blog/edcamps-the-new-professional-development-nicol-howard-sarah-thomas

Howard, N. R., Thomas, S., & Schaffer, R. (2018). *Closing the gap: Digital equity strategies for teacher prep programs*. Eugene, OR: ISTE.

Huggins, P. (2015, April 17). Wi-Fi helps bus discipline reports drop 70% for Huntsville City School; more Wi-Fi planned for 2015–16. AL. Retrieved from https://www.al.com/news/huntsville/index.ssf/2015/04/wi-fi_leads_to_70_drop_in_bus.html

International Society for Technology in Education. (2011). *ISTE Standards for Coaches*. Retrieved from https://www.iste.org/standards/for-coaches

International Society for Technology in Education. (2016). *ISTE Standards for Students*. Retrieved from https://www.iste.org/standards/for-students

International Society for Technology in Education. (2017). *ISTE Standards for Educators.* Retrieved from https://www.iste.org/standards/for-educators

International Technology and Engineering Educators Association. (n.d.). *Design process.* Retrieved from https://www.iteea.org/46855.aspx

Juarez, A., & Goyette, K. (2018). Break the walls down: 4C the future. Presentation at CUE Nevada, September 29, 2018. Retrieved from https://docs.google.com/presentation/d/1Z ZErFYfd81aa_2bIofuJsYicnHhd5Emtb_9ZBV0F03U/edit#slide=id.g43674b6cdc_2_117

Kahn, R., & Kellner, D. (2005). Reconstructing technoliteracy: A multiple literacies approach. *E-Learning and Digital Media, 2*(3), 238–251. https://doi.org/10.2304/elea.2005.2.3.4

Kajeet. (2018, April 2). *Kajeet and Google power rolling study halls.* Retrieved from https://www.kajeet.net/extracurricular/kajeet-google-power-rolling-student-halls

Keeley, B. (2007). *Human capital: How what you know shapes your life.* Paris: OECD.

Kinch, S. (2018, July 22). Rolling study halls: Bus Wi-Fi bridges "homework gap." *Wi-Fi NOW.* Retrieved from https://wifinowevents.com/news-and-blog/rolling-study-halls-add-wi-fi-to-buses-to-bridge-the-homework-gap

Krueger, K. & James, J. (March/April 2017). Digital equity: The civil rights issue of our time. *Principal.* Retrieved from https://www.naesp.org/principal-marchapril-2017-technology-all/digital-equity-civil-rights-issue-our-time

Lachney, M. (2017). Culturally responsive computing as brokerage: Toward asset building with education-based social movements. *Learning, Media and Technology, 42*(4), 420–439. https://doi.org/10.1080/17439884.2016.1211679

Landers, L. (2015, June 24). *Albemarle County Public School's Vince Scheivert named top CIO in nation* [Blog post]. Retrieved from https://cvilleinnovation.org/blog/leadership/cbic-board-member-shines-national-spotlight-on-charlottesville

Larson, S. (2017, November 17). FCC scales back broadband program for low-income Americans. *CNN.* Retrieved from https://money.cnn.com/2017/11/17/technology/fcc-lifeline-poor-americans/index.html

Lee, C. D. (2017). Toward a framework for culturally responsive design in multimedia computer environments: Cultural modeling as a case. In *Culture, Technology, and Development* (pp. 42–61). Psychology Press.

McLaughlin, C. (2016, April 20). The homework gap: The "cruelest part of the digital divide." *neaToday.* Retrieved from neatoday.org/2016/04/20/the-homework-gap

National Assessment of Educational Progress. (n.d.). Writing Assessment. Retrieved from https://nces.ed.gov/nationsreportcard/writing

Nazar, D. (2016, January 22). Wi-Fi-enabled school buses leave no child offline [Video]. *PBS News Hour.* Retrieved from https://www.pbs.org/newshour/show/wi-fi-enabled-school-buses-leave-no-child-offline

Project Tomorrow. (2018). *Professional learning for teachers new demands need new approaches.* Retrieved from https://tomorrow.org/speakup/speakup-2017-professional-learning-for-teachers-may-2018.html

Randhawa, S. (2017, October 31). WiFi–equipped school buses help students get online. *CNN.* Retrieved from https://edition.cnn.com/2017/10/31/tech/homework-gap/index.html

Reich, J. & Ito, M. (2017). *From good intentions to real outcomes: Equity by design in learning technologies.* Irvine, CA: Digital Media and Learning Research Hub.

Ryerse, M. & Berkeley, M. (2018, October 17). Who you know: Relationships are an undervalued asset for students. *Getting Smart*. Retrieved from https://www.gettingsmart.com/2018/10/who-you-know-relationships-are-an-undervalued-asset-for-students

Sampson, R. (2015, March 10). Personalized PD: What teachers really want. *Medium*. Retrieved from https://medium.com/@randallsampson/what-teachers-really-want-a3fcf516dc95

Schlosser, N. (2017, February 28). IC Bus Innovation Summit envisions future of the school bus. *School Bus Fleet*. Retrieved from https://www.schoolbusfleet.com/news/721219/ic-bus-innovation-summit-envisions-future-of-the-school-bus

Scott, K. A., Sheridan, K. M., & Clark, K. (2015). Culturally responsive computing: A theory revisited. *Learning, Media and Technology, 40*(4), 412–436. https://doi.org/10.1080/17439884.2014.924966

Scott, K. A., & White, M. A. (2013). COMPUGIRLS' standpoint: Culturally responsive computing and its effect on girls of color. *Urban Education, 48*(5), 657–681. https://doi.org/10.1177/0042085913491219

Siefer, A. (2015, September 8). Community-based solutions for Lifeline broadband [Blog post]. *Digital Inclusion News*. Retrieved from https://www.digitalinclusion.org/blog/2015/9/8/community-based-solutions-lifeline

Simmons, T. (2017). Going beyond the walls: Part II. In *EduMatch: Snapshot in Education 2017, Volume 1* (pp. 241–255). Alexandria, VA: EduMatch.

Spring, J. (2018). *The American school: From the Puritans to the Trump era*. New York: Routledge.

Stoeckl, S. (2018, February 22). Students use grief, passion, technology to create a movement. *ISTE*. Retrieved from https://www.iste.org/explore/articleDetail?articleid=2149

T-Mobile. (n.d.). *EmpowerED*. Retrieved from
    https://uncarrier.t-mobile.com/empowered

Thomas, S. (n.d.). *Designing with passion.* Retrieved from
    https://docs.google.com/forms/d/e/1FAIpQLSe_
    iNUpLynWISe1QRgv3wgLJpgq_vhu0F9-O5adDf__0skxzw/
    viewform

Thomas, S. (2017, June 14). Teacher empowerment reflected
    in new Educator Standards. *ISTE.* Retrieved from
    https://www.iste.org/explore/articleDetail?articleid=
    995&category=Empowered-Learner&article=

Thomas, S. (2018, March 4). *Empathy vs. "compassion" (aka
    "dangerous minds" et).* Retrieved from https://medium.com/
    sarahdateechur/empathy-vs-compassion-aka-dangerous-
    minds-et-7019b331d9be

Udall, T. (2018, May 24). *Text—S.2958—115th Congress (2017-2018): A
    bill to require the Federal Communications Commission to make the
    provision of Wi-Fi access on school buses eligible for E-Rate support.*
    Retrieved from https://www.congress.gov/bill/115th-congress/
    senate-bill/2958/text

U.S. Department of Education, Institute of Educational Sciences.
    (2012). National Assessment of Educational Progress (NAEP),
    2011 Writing Assessment. Washington D.C.: U.S. Dept.
    of Education, National Center for Education Statistics.
    Retrieved from https://nces.ed.gov/nationsreportcard/pubs/
    main2011/2012470.aspx

U.S. Department of Education, National Center for Education
    Statistics. (2009). Table 426: Percent of home computer users
    using specific applications, by selected characteristics: 1997
    and 2003. In U.S. Department of Education, National Center
    for Education Statistics (Ed.), *Digest of Education Statistics* (2009
    ed.). Retrieved from https://nces.ed.gov/programs/digest/d04/
    tables/dt04_426.asp

U.S. Department of Education, National Center for Education Statistics. (2016). Table 702.10: Percentage of children ages 3 to 18 living in households with a computer, by type of computer and selected child and family characteristics: Selected years, 2010 through 2015. In U.S. Department of Education, National Center for Education Statistics (Ed.), *Digest of Education Statistics* (2016 ed.). Retrieved from https://nces.ed.gov/programs/digest/d16/tables/dt16_702.10.asp

U.S. Department of Education, Office of Educational Technology. (2017). National Education Technology Plan. Washington D.C.: U.S. Dept. of Education, Office of Educational Technology. Retrieved from https://tech.ed.gov/netp

van Dijk, J., & Hacker, K. (2003). The digital divide as a complex and dynamic phenomenon. *Information Society, 19*(4), 315–326. https://doi.org/10.1080/01972240309487

Vega, V. (2013, January 3). Teacher development research review: Keys to educator success [Blog post]. *Edutopia: A George Lucas Educational Foundation.* Retrieved from https://www.edutopia.org/teacher-development-research-keys-success

Warschauer, M., Knobel, M., & Stone, L. (2004). Technology and equity in schooling: Deconstructing the digital divide. *Educational policy, 18*(4), 562–588. https://doi.org/10.1177/0895904804266469

INDEX

Page numbers followed by "t" and "f" indicate tables and figures.

Your Opinion Matters
Tell Us How We're Doing!

Your feedback helps ISTE create the best possible resources for teaching and learning in the digital age. Share your thoughts with the community or tell us how we're doing!

You Can:

- Write a review at amazon.com or barnesandnoble.com.

- Mention this book on social media and follow ISTE on Twitter @iste, Facebook @ISTEconnects or Instagram @isteconnects

- Email us at books@iste.org with your questions or comments.